Endorsements

"I have been waiting for this book for a very long time. It seems like ages. This book is not just about Ron's 25-plus years of ministry with kids in hard places. In many ways, it's more about how ministry to young people has broken and shaped Ron's heart for God and for the proclaiming of the good news in hard places. If you work with young people who are marginalized and forgotten, you will find yourself at home here and you will breathe a deep "Amen." You may not know it, but you have been waiting for this book for a very long time! Finally, a book that is for you! Enjoy!"
—*Lina Thompson, national director of Capacity Building and Community Development at World Vision US Programs*

"Ron Ruthruff writes from his heart and shares more than two decades of working and learning about life from street-involved youth. These lessons demonstrate an integration of faith and social work and illustrate at a practical level how Ron and others sought to support these vulnerable youth. Ron offers readers an opportunity to reflect on their own practice and philosophy, to examine what motivates them to serve, and how to serve more effectively. This book is a testament to Ron as an inspirational individual who continues to examine himself and the world around him, in order to be a more effective agent of social change."
—*Tracy W. Harachi, MSW, PhD, associate professor, School of Social Work, University of Washington*

"Ruthruff passes on lessons learned at the seminary of the sidewalk. These lessons are not just sprinkled with the color of the street for creditability, but permeated with the pigment of a life spent bearing witness in hard places. Dr. Ron is no ivory-tower observer; he is a street-level scholar who has penned a prophetic book that is powerfully practical."
—*Joel Kiekintveld, executive director, Parachutes Teen Club & Resource Center, Anchorage, Alaska, www.parachutesalaska.com*

The Least of These

of These

Lessons Learned from Kids on the Street

Ron Ruthruff

NEW HOPE
P U B L I S H E R S
Birmingham, Alabama

New Hope® Publishers
P. O. Box 12065
Birmingham, AL 35202-2065
www.newhopepublishers.com

Library of Congress Cataloging-in-Publication Data

Ruthruff, Ron, 1962-
The least of these : lessons learned from kids on the street / Ron Ruthruff.
    p. cm.
  Includes bibliographical references.
  ISBN-13: 978-1-59669-272-5 (jhc)
  ISBN-10: 1-59669-272-3
1. Church work with youth with social disabilities--Washington--Seattle.
I. Title.
  BV4447.R88 2010
  259'.230869420973--dc22

                              2010026733

Scripture quotations marked *The Message* are taken from *The Message* by Eugene H. Peterson. Copyright © 1993, 1994, 1995, 1996, 2000, 2001, 2002. Used by permission of NavPress Publishing Group.

Scripture quotations marked NRSV are taken from the New Revised Standard Version Bible, copyright 1989, by the Division of Christian Education of the National Council of the Churches of Christ in the U.S.A. Used by permission. All rights reserved.

Scripture quotations marked NKJV are taken from the New King James Version. Copyright © 1982 by Thomas Nelson, Inc. Used by permission. All rights reserved.

Scripture quotations marked NIV are taken from the HOLY BIBLE, NEW INTERNATIONAL VERSION®. NIV®. Copyright © 1973, 1978, 1984 by International Bible Society. Used by permission of Zondervan. All rights reserved.

ISBN-10: 1-59669-272-3
ISBN-13: 978-1-59669-272-5
N104135 • 1010 • 3M1

Dedication

To Linda

My wife and partner

I have served with you our entire married life. You challenge me to live out all that I preach and together we work prayerfully for justice and beauty in this world. You truly are a coauthor on this project and I can never express how much you mean to me. You exemplify grace, hospitality, and love, and I am forever grateful that you are my wife.

Contents

Acknowledgments

To my sons, Ben and Clayton
You are the best. Both of you have embraced the call to love and speak truth in the world, in your own way. You are better at what I love than I am and every day you make me proud. Ben, keep loving kids as though your life depends on it. Clayton, keep speaking truth to power.

To my mother, Esther Ruthruff
You turned 90 as this manuscript went to print. You worked as a nursing assistant the entire time you raised me. I watched you carry bed pans, feed the elderly, and mend their clothes. No college taught me more about serving than you did. Thank you for your example of love to the least of these.

To my church, Emerald City Bible Fellowship
As a multicultural witness to God's incredible love, you have taught me enough for another book. I love that you love me and celebrate the gifts my family brings to this community.

To my pastor, Harvey Drake
You have led this vision for a community that crosses boundaries and breaks down barriers.

To my professors at Gordon Conwell Theological Seminary, and Pepperdine University
Thank you. You gave me a love for the biblical text that can be lived out on the street.

To all those men who have poured into me
I have learned that we must be mentored and must mentor in return. Thank you for shaping my theology and teaching me how to serve.

To Pastor Dale Sewall, thank you.
You are my dear friend and big brother.

To the young brothers who call me mentor
I am humbled but honored to be in your life. You have poured into me and I into you and we serve in the city because we do it together. I wish I could mention you all but you know who you are!

To the staff, volunteers, and board of New Horizons Ministries
You let me love and serve with you for more than 25 years—thank you. Your lives bear witness to these stories; I could never claim them as my own.

To the former executive director, Rita Nussli, whom I served with for 22 years, thank you.
You always told me the truth, challenged me, and taught me how to lead. You are one of the finest leaders I have ever known.

A big thank you to my publisher, and all my new friends at New Hope Publishers.
I am humbled by your belief in me and your support of this project. You all have been more helpful than I would have ever imagined.

To the kids on the streets
No words can express my gratefulness to you. I have walked with you and you have given me this book. I have had the privilege to love you on the street, in jail, in the hospital—and you have loved me back. You have let me into your lives, and your death. Your names would fill all the pages of this book. God will not forget you or forsake you. Some day, when the God of the universe redeems all things to Himself and all that is not good is gone, we will rejoice together in a family that will never end. I love you.

Some of the names and places
in this text have been altered
in order to respect the privacy
of those who are part of
the true stories here.

Foreword

Intersecting and Walking with "the Least"

I met Ron Ruthruff at a New Horizons volunteer training in 1986. One of my "heroin-addicted clients" at a group home for teenage girls recruited me to teach the "Drug and Alcohol Addictions" portion of the training. She introduced me to then-training coordinator Susan Jouflas, saying, "You two crazy Christians should meet." Since Susan and I both were hanging out with street kids. I decided to attend the entire training, and sat mesmerized as a radical young man with a mullet haircut and one blind eye told stories about who street kids are. Within the year, I became the executive director for New Horizons and began a 22-year ministry partnership with Ron and his wife, Linda.

Each night of outreach to the streets brought new relationships. Drop-in, with all its laughter and craziness, taught us about living lives of hope. Follow-up activities made it clear: the best therapy is often accomplished while shooting pool or playing foosball.

From the beginning, I *knew* that God had called Ron to teach others what street kids teach us—and I began asking Ron, "When will you write your book?"

As Ron told the kids' stories, profound truths lay bare; truth about justice, mercy, and the essential need to be taught by the "least of these." We were experiencing Jesus as we lived our lives in community with the homeless street kids whom we were serving.

Ron began attending community college and his assignment papers reflected the lessons he was learning on the streets—as much as what he was learning from his professors. Serving full time at New Horizons, Ron completed his BA, his masters, and finally his doctorate in "Complex Urban Settings," at Gordon Conwell. His education has reinforced to him that lessons learned from the youth he has served best express the mystery of God's incarnate presence and the transformative power of hope.

As I read through Ron's words here, I know he has captured what he has been learning and teaching for some 25 years, and continues to know and teach:

> Don't walk past the homeless, the poor, the addicted—these modern-day lepers—without stopping to listen, and to see God's children with clarity, for they can be our greatest teachers. When we truly see them, we will have met Jesus.

May you experience the sorrow, joy, laughter, love, hope, and, most of all, the gift of our shared community as you journey through these pages with the least of these.

Rita Nussli, MSW
www.SoulFormation.org

"God himself taught us to meet one another
as God has met us in Christ."
—DIETRICH BONHOEFFER, *Life Together*

1

New Lessons
to Learn
Together

W E FIRST VISITED THE DROP-IN CENTER IN THE FALL of 1982. Late at night after a concert in Seattle, my friend Eric walked with me past a darkened storefront on Union Street. We peeked inside as Eric said, "I want you to check out this place. Too bad they're not open. It's run by New Horizons Ministries. They call this Saint Dismas Center." I later discovered tradition claims Dismas as patron saint of thieves. Some believe Dismas was the thief hanging on a cross next to Jesus who asked Jesus to remember him (Luke 23:32–43). That thief reminds us that there's hope in seemingly hopeless places, and it's never too late to share it.

➡ ERIC knew I had spent the summer of 1980 working with chronic alcoholics and addicts at a San Francisco mission. I loved the city and everyone knew it. As we hung outside the Saint Dismas Center, my friend continued to talk about New Horizons. "They're really cool Christians who come from a lot of different churches and serve all the street kids that hang out downtown. They're really professional too; like, you have to be trained to volunteer with them. They really get to know the kids. They go to court with them, visit them at detention, and just help them. It's a great place. You would love it!" As we looked into the window of the dilapidated building, I could see the silhouette of a pool table and some couches. Even in the dark, it was obvious the couches had seen better days. Gradually we moved on up the street, talking about the concert.

➡️ In the spring of 1983, another friend, **John**, was doing a Bible school internship—with New Horizons Ministries! John suggested I think about volunteering too. He offered to take me to the drop-in center to check things out. I explained how Eric had introduced me to the place, and then said, "It sounds like a great place, but I have plenty going on in my life." I was working at a cabinet shop, playing in a band, and loving life in my one-bedroom rental for $85 a month. John asked me to come down to the center for one night—"just one night"—to serve dinner. As he begged, I began to reconsider. "OK, just one night." I thought, *One night couldn't hurt, and besides, Eric would laugh at the strange coincidence that introduced me to this place twice in one year.*

On a chilly Saturday night, John and I traveled from my little "mansion" about 50 miles north of the city to Saint Dismas Center, 1312 Second Avenue. About 6:30 in the evening, we met a few other 20-somethings who were volunteering. They seemed normal but definitely not street-savvy. With my long hair, sleeveless T-shirt, and a past, I knew I brought something new to the place; I thought I was cool. We began planning the evening. We would first pray, then be on the streets until about 9:00 P.M., invite kids to a meal, come back, open the drop-in center, and serve dinner until about 10:00 P.M. Amen! Enough praying! I was ready.

We were not on the streets for more than 15 minutes when a young woman, about 17 years old, walked up to John and me. Frantic, she started her story midsentence.

➡ "BRENDA, this is my friend Ron." John tried to start the conversation with some introductions, but she completely ignored him. She kept throwing out all these problems. She had just pulled a trick. Her boyfriend had taken all her money and had left her to get high. She called her mom, only to find out that Mom's new boyfriend wanted Brenda out of the house. Brenda said she hated the shelters. "Everyone steals, and they are all stupid kids—dumb, not street-wise." Now she had no choice but to turn another trick for a place to stay. I had heard enough. I told her that this might be the way it was, but definitely not the way it was supposed to be. "God has—!" She quickly interrupted me. "Who the hell are you?" she exclaimed. I realized that she must not have heard John introduce me. I thought he might jump in and let her know who I was and assure her that my experience warranted me getting involved in helping her. But John didn't reintroduce me. He listened to Brenda and then quietly began to ask her a few questions.

Looking back, I don't think Brenda was trying to discredit my street knowledge, even though she would have been justified in doing so—totally. I think she believed that I lacked credibility. All she saw was some young outsider trying to tell her that the problems she'd been wrestling with for the past how many years could be solved in a sentence or two. My first lesson in crisis counseling was, and continues to be, that when people are in crisis and struggling with complex problems, the last thing they want, or need, is a quick answer. Imagine the frustration a person in crisis would feel if a counselor said, "Oh, that problem you've been struggling with is so easy. What you have not been able to answer in a month I can answer in 35 seconds. Boy, are you stupid."

John listened to Brenda, then asked her questions that highlighted her strengths and her resources. He asked Brenda if she had been in this spot before, and what she had done then. John taught me a lot. Brenda taught me more. If I am going to be with people, and be of any help, I need to get to know them first. I need to know where they've come from, their problems, and their strengths. I also must allow them to know me. "You don't know anything!" Brenda screamed. She was right; I didn't. But I do now, because the kids on the street have taught me and continue to do so.

As I think about all I have learned over the years from the kids on the streets and the incredible people I have served with, I am truly humbled. I have discovered that God's light shines most brightly in the darkest places. I have also discovered that the young people who look like they need the most help have been my most significant teachers. That the most broken people in the world allow the greater community of faith to live out what was manifested in the life of Jesus, and that God commands His people to be people who bear witness to His kindness, mercy, justice, and humility.

I also have learned that my social location—that is, my place in this world as a privileged Anglo North American male, can actually hinder my ability to see and serve. Power, privilege, and resources can actually impede my service because they limit my ability to learn and listen. Those of us born into privilege tend to think we have the answers because we have all the resources. We cannot minister effectively with this attitude. We must pour ourselves into service even as we pour out our preconceived notions of the people we serve.

Buried Treasure

Dietrich Bonhoeffer said in his book *Life Together*, "God himself taught us to meet one another as God has met us in Christ." Bonhoeffer wrote this book while Hitler reigned in Nazi Germany, trying to exterminate everyone different from himself. In the midst of an oppressive and persecuting climate, Bonhoeffer encouraged the Church to see Jesus in all of the people different from themselves. He taught that the Jesus in ourselves is minimized when we become exclusive in our social location. Our class, culture, ethnicity, and gender all hinder us from seeing the complete Jesus. Bonhoeffer encouraged the Church to listen with the ears of God before speaking the words of God. Imagine a community of faith that listens and learns from each other. Imagine a missiology that revolves around listening and learning as much as teaching and speaking. What would it mean if we listened and learned as we served the widow, orphan, and stranger?

What would it mean if we listened and learned as we served the widow, orphan, and stranger?

On that night so many years ago, John and I made our way back to Second and Union. The drop-in center was dimly lit, and a few kids had lined up, waiting to be invited in. They waited to warm themselves in a building that had no heat. New Horizons Ministries' drop-in center was a condemned storefront surrounded by abandoned buildings on each side. Above the drop-in center was an abandoned hotel that was home to an occasional transient and large city rats. I walked into this place that night, and it became my seminary. The kids and other people I met became my professors. I didn't know anything. I didn't know who they were or where they came from. I didn't even know who I was or where I came from, but I was about to learn. I walked into New Horizons for one night—and never left.

Years had passed since that first visit in 1983, when I sat in a coffee shop with a woman from Lagos, Nigeria. She was studying social work at the University of Washington. She wanted to learn more about street children in the United States, so she asked if I could meet her for coffee to discuss the work of New Horizons Ministries. As I told her about the tragedy of America's street kids—the abuse, neglect, violence, addiction, mental health issues, and suicide, she looked at me with tears in her eyes. "The richest place in Seattle is not the house of Bill Gates. It's the graves of your young people. In these graves are buried unrealized dreams and untapped potential. There is a treasure buried with your kids."

If this book is anything, it's an effort to find that treasure. Not only treasure that is buried with the kids whose lives have been cut short on the street. Treasure lies in kids whose lives have been hidden behind the rough exterior necessary for street survival. I hold strongly to the belief that kids on the street see God in amazing ways simply because God is close to those who suffer. These resilient young people have been, in one way or another, pushed out of their homes. They have lived in garbage cans and abandoned buildings. They sell drugs and sell their young bodies to survive on the street. The families that they create on the street display the same brokenness as the families they run from. The streets create a cycle of pain and discomfort, followed by temporary relief, followed by more pain and discomfort. But, in the middle of all this, these amazing young people continue, through their courage, resiliency, and prayerfulness, to reveal the story of God.

*If my father and mother forsake me,
the L*ORD *will take me up.*
—PSALM 27:10

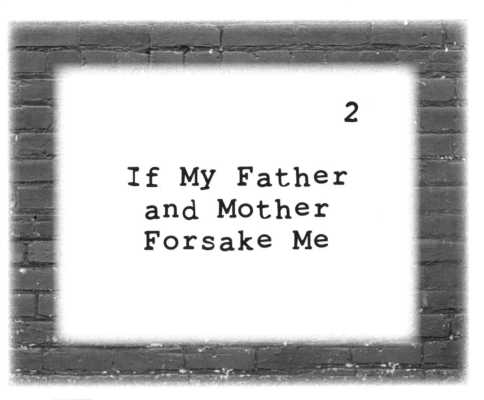

2

If My Father
and Mother
Forsake Me

THE OVERWHELMING MAJORITY OF KIDS ON THE STREET ARE running from severe family dysfunction. According to the National Runaway Hotline, between 1 and 2 million youth run away each year. Why such a discrepancy? The young people leaving their homes are running literally and figuratively to the streets. They don't stand still to be counted. In the greater Seattle area, an estimated 5,000 youth run away from home each year. Both nationally and in the Seattle area, about 50 percent of these runaways return home. An additional 25 percent of these young people have their needs met through service-delivery agencies. The remaining 25 percent of runaway youth, approximately 1,500 to 2,000 in King County, begin a journey to hard-core street life.

Through my experience of working with kids since 1983, and through collaboration with others who have done the same work, I've learned that the major driving force for young people ending up on the streets is sexual abuse, neglect, and violence in their homes. Folklore credits Mark

Twain as saying, "The biggest mistake children make is the parents they choose." I believe the streets feel safer to the kids than the communities and families from which they are running. These kids are running *from* a bad situation rather than *to* the streets. Since 1978, New Horizons Ministries has been helping many of these runaway, homeless, and street-involved young people.

Experts estimate that almost half of street-involved youth are refugees or runaways from the state's foster care system. They identify three primary reasons why the overcrowded system does not work for kids:

1. **Multiple placements.** Youth leave homes where trust has been violated, or they are taken from places of the most extreme abuse and neglect. Bouncing from place to place erodes the child's capacity to trust adults.
2. **Sibling separation.** Having a brother or sister placed in a different home can be devastating to a child. However, the system is not always able to keep families together.
3. **Lack of cultural understanding among foster care providers.** Youth of color are often placed into neighborhoods, schools, and families with different lifestyles. Food is different, communication styles are different, and youth see no faces in authority that look like their own.

For these reasons, and many others, youth lose faith in the ability of the foster care system to meet their needs, and they run. They run to the streets looking for—and hoping to find—something better.

Kids on the street have their social and economic needs met though street-developed relationships. Petty crime, prostitution, and drug sales become their way to survive. These activities contribute to their social status as well as their economic needs. Kids on the street are street-wise, mature experientially, and system-savvy; yet, they are developmentally and emotionally immature due to childhood trauma and family dysfunction. The kids are survivors. They have grown up with, and run away from, insanity. Their resiliency is remarkable.

Homeless young people long for community and join street families and gang-type groups. Many times these groups mirror the brokenness of past family relationships. Kids on the street have lost faith in the dominant culture's ability to parent them and to address their needs as maturing children and adolescents. All of this is a result of abuse and neglect. People who work with this population argue that between 60 percent and 90 percent of all homeless adolescents have suffered severe physical and sexual abuse, most often by family members and caregivers. This high percentage of abuse is not surprising if we consider the widely held belief that one in four women and one in eight men in the general population have reported being sexually abused.

Hitting the Streets

➡ JERMAINE'S mom was only 15 years old when he was born. Social workers with Child Protective Services were at the hospital at the time. His memories of his mom were visits on the weekends. His housing was provided by the state foster care system, and as an adolescent, he lived in state-funded group homes. These are the homes he remembers. When Jermaine and I talked about his family memories, he always began by asking, "Which one?" When he reflected on his past, he said that even at a young age he knew he could not trust the various people who served as his surrogate family. He told about one foster family that told him his room was in the basement, and that's where he was to remain unless he was invited into the rest of the house. Jermaine was 14 when he hit the streets.

He was tired of living in neighborhoods where he was the only kid of color, tired of being a "foster kid," and tired of feeling stupid when he moved through four middle schools in two years. So when most teenagers are entering into a new phase of independence with a safety net of family and community, Jermaine headed into adolescence and adulthood alone. Clearly, he believed it was better to face the pilgrimage to adulthood on his own. Jermaine, like many of the 14-year-olds we see in the drop-in center, was developmentally immature, but he had experience well beyond his years.

A child not getting their needs met as a child, but living though experiences far beyond their age creates a paradox that significantly hinders healthy maturation. It's no surprise that a teenager—no matter how resilient he or she is—after surviving multiple foster placements, changing middle schools, and living in culturally foreign neighborhoods, would choose to face adolescence alone.

➡ SUSAN was a beautiful young woman who dressed with a hint of punk and had extremely good social skills. Every volunteer loved this high-functioning kid. She was from New England and very "East Coast." She was a good conversationalist, a good activity leader, and ... a young woman involved in prostitution. She talked about her involvement in prostitution candidly, without feeling or emotion. One day the timing was right, and I asked, "Susan, why prostitution?" She looked at me, absent of any emotion. "Why not sell it? My dad got it for free." Her voice trailed off as if she was thinking deeply about how to place blame on herself rather than her father, hoping somehow to make sense of it all. She remembered her home being perfect on the outside. Her father had a lucrative job; her mother was a stay-at-home mom; and her brother was a star athlete. She remembered that her mother and father lived separate lives, but there is no way to tell what led her father to cross the sacred boundaries between daughter and father and put her through years of sexual abuse.

➡ **DAVID** grew up in the housing projects of South Seattle. He remembered his mom and her boyfriends selling drugs out of their two-bedroom home. His bedroom door was near the front door. After dark, after he was in bed, David heard the door opening and closing over and over again. As he grew older, he realized customers were coming in and out of the house, buying dope. He was 12 years old when his mother gave him LSD. She told him, "If you're going to 'trip,' you might as well do it at home." He remembers customers trading cribs and car seats for dope. His mother traded the commodities to her grandchildren or sold them to the neighbors for cash. By age 15, David was immersed in the street life without ever leaving home.

> After dark, after he was in bed, David heard the door opening and closing over and over again.

➡ **DONNY** was six-feet tall and 13 years old. The first question he was asked by new friends or acquaintances was, "You play basketball?" Donny didn't. He told me that story over the phone. Most of our friendship was established over the phone—he was locked up a lot. In our phone conversations, Donny and I would talk about everything from theology and relationships, to how he ended up on the streets and incarcerated.

One day as we talked, he simply started to tell me the story of his growing up. He really didn't remember much before seventh grade. However, he remembered enough to speak politely of his father and mother. "They loved me," he would say, trying to excuse the stories that followed. During his early adolescence, he remembered not fitting in. "I was six-feet tall and couldn't play basketball." Donny struggled with a very normal adolescent dilemma. He wanted to make important decisions but felt completely unprepared to do so. So he searched for something that would make him look important. Basketball was out. So, as he walked to school one morning and noticed the leaves in shades of green and brown that lay upon his path, it seemed obvious—he should sell pot!

An incredibly difficult reality is that, for some kids in some neighborhoods, basketball, acting, and dope sales are seen as the only ways to elevate their economic status. Kids watch TV and want to imitate the "cool" guys selling dope. They see characters earning status and power and think that selling drugs may be a good option. Eugene Rivers, a pastor in a tough Boston neighborhood has said, that many kids have limited or no contact with a dad, and might see a pastor or mentor once a week. However, they see the dope man every day. Donny, with all the forethought of a 13-year-old kid, gathered up the leaves, crushed them into a plastic bag, and rambled off to school. He was probably there two hours before one of his classmates got wind of the drug sales. By the end of the day, he was in the principal's office.

Donny was judged on his intentions, not the authenticity of substance, and was expelled. His adopted dad was furious. The man was an older German immigrant who believed that if the boy wanted to be a drug dealer, he should be treated like one. Donny's dad threw him into the family's station wagon and took him to juvenile detention. Donny remembers trying to tell his dad that he wasn't selling pot, but merely maple leaves. Donny wasn't old enough to analyze his own motivation, but he was mature enough to realize it was about something other than drug sales. Donny's dad would hear none of it. Soon after taking him into juvenile detention, Donny's dad was told that they couldn't detain his son. He had, in their words, committed no crime. A frustrated father reluctantly took his son back home. Donny ended up back in school, but something had changed that day. The rest of the year was uneventful, and Donny completed seventh grade. That summer the family decided that Donny could go to a local church summer camp. His Christian counselor allegedly introduced him to marijuana. Ironic that the first time Donny ever got stoned was at a Christian summer camp. Within 15 minutes, he was caught, and by the end of the day, he was sent home. As Donny told the story, it sounded like some self-fulfilling prophecy. All of his father's assumptions were confirmed. His father once again took him to juvenile detention. Donny remembers the look on the face of the young man at the front desk. The man couldn't believe a father, in utter frustration, was trying so hard to get his son arrested. "I will not take him home!" Donny's father proclaimed. The man at the front desk had to switch hats rather quickly. He tried his best to be a social worker in order to bring some element of peace to the chaotic moment. He told Donny's father about a shelter run by the YMCA. It was a place for kids who were not able to go home. Donny really doesn't remember what happened next. He remembers walking into the YMCA alone and asking about a shelter. He would not see his family again until manhood. Donny, in the middle of all this confusion and beginning adolescence, drifted toward the streets and later toward the crimes that would help him survive.

At age 19, Donny had spent as many days locked up as he had days on the street. I first connected with him when one of my co-workers was planning for a leave of absence. She was getting married and thought Donny might call from jail while she was gone. She asked if I'd fill in for her and take his collect calls. Shortly after that, while I was working in the drop-in center, a tall, lanky kid walked in. He was traveling light and walked into New Horizons with only an old bowling bag, which he used to carry his change of clothes. We had only talked a short time when I realized it was Donny. An even shorter time after that, I realized he'd escaped from jail. Now, *escape* is a loaded word. Really, he had just walked away from a prison work-release program. The consequence that undoubtedly lay before him when he was eventually caught was another long-term prison sentence.

For the next few days, Donny and I discussed theology, life, and the implications of him turning himself in. Donny was terrified; he had spent a lot of time behind bars and the thought of going back of his own volition was unfathomable. But soon the law of averages caught up with him, and he was arrested. Donny spent most of the next 15 years behind bars. During that time, he became a Christian and spoke fondly of the a television preachers whom he met via satellite and watched on TV daily. Our friendship grew through letters and collect phone calls. Donny still speaks fondly of the men and women who came into his prison room via satellite.

One of the greatest things about working at a place like New Horizons is that the approach is extremely relational. If kids lack relationship and community then relationship and community must surround every element of an organization's service delivery model. This value has led New Horizons volunteers and staff to visit kids in the hospital, celebrate their graduation from drug treatment, and be with them at the birth of their children. This is the theological principle of the first chapter of John's Gospel. *"In the beginning was the Word, and the Word was with God, and the Word was God.... and the Word became flesh and dwelt among us"* (John 1:1, 14 NKJV). My own boys say that God chose to hang out in our neighborhood. This idea of the incarnation and God becoming flesh led me and my co-workers at New Horizons to many interesting places.

A Pilgrimage to Vacaville

Donny doesn't remember much about New Horizons' "programs," but what he does remember are the people who reached out to him. No ministry or agency—just relationships. He remembers the staff and volunteers who remembered his birthday and, when he was locked up, sent him cards at Christmastime. During one memorable conversation, he told me that he had saved every card and photo that I had sent him. We wrote a lot, talked a lot on the phone, and, on a few special occasions, I was able to visit with him in a few different prisons. I remember one visit to Vacaville specifically.

We wrote a lot, talked a lot on the phone, and, on a few special occasions, I was able to visit with him in a few different prisons.

Vacaville is an institution in the California prison system. Its formal name is the California Medical Facility. Anyone with a long-term illness or who is chronically or terminally ill is sent there. In many ways, it's a modern-day leper colony.

Now, I know how to do a jail visit—I've done those hundreds of times. If you're visiting someone locked up in the county jail, where a person is detained less than a year, your visit consists of looking at each other through a glass window, and the conversation is limited to talking on a phone that might or might not work. When visiting at a prison, an institution that keeps a person 366 days or more, you must first go through a background check and get on an official visiting list. However, you get a real face-to-face visit—two to three hours of personal contact in a day room, especially equipped with vending machines that have the ability to provide a virtual feast for the inmate you are visiting. You make some microwave popcorn, buy a few candy bars, a soft drink or two, and then magic happens—it's Thanksgiving dinner—prison-style.

Because I'm familiar with the drill, anytime I visit a young person at an institution, I call ahead. I did this prior to planning my trip to visit Don (now grown, that's what we call him). I knew all the appropriate questions. I verified I was on his visiting list, asked how many photos I could bring in with me, and how much money I could bring in for the essential vending machine snacks. I was in San Francisco teaching a class, and rented a car to make the two-hour pilgrimage to Vacaville. I followed the rules meticulously. I brought no wallet. All I had with me was my driver's license, $20 in change, and a $10 bill for gas. Oh yes, and one more thing. What to wear is always a concern with a prison visit. You want to look professional so you don't get treated as bad as an inmate or an inmate's family. But you don't want to wear some suit and look like a federal agent. I thought I did pretty well. I put on a black T-shirt, a denim shirt, and a nice pair of jeans. My belt and shoes were black, always a good choice when you're trying to accessorize denim.

So I headed to Vacaville. I looked casual yet conservative, professional but hip. I had enough change for the feast and my ID. I carried the limit of seven photos, including pictures of my family and the NHM staff. It is always stressful to wait to go into a concrete structure with razor wire. Gun turrets don't make me feel safe. My ID was checked, my money was counted, and my photos inspected. All that was left was the metal detector. The very polite prison guard looked at me and said very kindly, "Sir, do you realize you're dressed inappropriately?" *Dressed inappropriately?* I questioned inwardly. *Did she realize how long I spent thinking about my outfit? I was looking good!* "You can't wear denim into the prison," she patiently explained. "Can you go home and change?" I explained that home was 1,500 miles away and that my hotel was two hours away. I had no money except my $20 in change. "Where is the closest Target?" I asked. Not one close, but she gave me directions to another prison. She assured me that they had a clothing trailer. I would have to line up with the other rule breakers, turn in my civilian clothes, and be issued an appropriate outfit to borrow for my visit. Boy, did I get an outfit.

I lined up, the only man, with all of the inmate's girl-friends and wives. I made it to the front of the line and was told to state my shirt size and waist size. *What about my inseam?* I thought. *Isn't length important?* Obviously it wasn't, because I was given a gold pair of Britannia bell-bottoms, about an inch too short. They also gave me a yellow T-shirt that looked like it had been donated by a California road crew. I turned in my own clothes and was told that if I didn't return each item I had borrowed, that I would not get my own clothes back. "I will return them!" I promised. So I headed back to Vacaville. I was now dressed *appropriately.* I was heading into the California prison system, and I looked like some sort of daisy or sunbeam who worked for highway construction.

I walked into the visiting room and there stood Don wearing a blue denim shirt and blue jeans, California prison state-issued. Don looked at me and immediately began to laugh. I told him the story, and we laughed some more. They didn't tell me that every inmate wears blue denim. The last thing that the prison authorities wanted was iden-tity confusion between the inmates and the visitors. Don and I sat down with microwave popcorn, soft drinks, and candy bars. I showed him photos of life outside Vacaville and quickly forgot that a few years had passed since we had talked face-to-face. Don and I never had a tough time making conversation. He talked to me about all of the craziness and illness of inmates in the California Medical Facility. He spoke with compassion of his fellow inmates who felt so isolated, and talked of the prisoners with AIDS who were incarcerated and forgotten—really just left to die.

We got to the place in the prison visit where I asked him how he was holding up. He said, "I've been in the hole (solitary confinement)." *What had he done?* I thought. He read my mind. "Too many books in my cell. I had a Bible, a *Strong's Bible Concordance*, and a third book. They caught me reading Gordon Fee's *How to Read the Bible for All It's Worth.*" This "heinous" crime had gotten him a few months in the hole. The worst part of the story is that it was my fault. I sent him the book.

He assured me that the hole had not been too bad. "I have been memorizing Scripture. I memorized Romans and Galatians."

I asked him, "Which verses?"

He replied, "They're letters, right? I thought you should memorize the whole thing!" Don had spent each day in the hole memorizing Scripture. He'd have breakfast, read the verses, pace the 4-by-8-foot cell, and then memorize. He'd eat lunch, do push-ups, pace the 4-by-8-foot cell, read the verses, and then memorize. He'd then eat dinner, do push-ups, read some more verses, and then memorize. Rather than his time alone in his cell driving him crazy, it was building something altogether different—something incredible. The Bible was completely hidden in Don's mind and heart.

For the next two hours of our visit, we discussed Romans—from Don's memory—not mine. We talked about the psychological struggle of chapter 7 and the spiritual fulfillment of chapter 8. We discussed chapter 12 and the meaning of presenting your body as a living sacrifice. We contemplated this together. I no longer was aware that I was sitting in the visitor's center wearing yellow from my neck to almost my ankles. Don mentioned that he and some other Christians were trying to organize a program in which each prisoner who is close to death gets another inmate to sit with him. "No one should die alone," Don said. Don was reading the Scripture, loving his neighbor, and living out the gospel, in a hellish place.

Treasure Found

I walked into the prison that day thinking that I had a lot to give. I walked in as clergy, a social worker, and an urban ministry practitioner. However, something transforming happened to me that day in the visiting room. Leslie Newbigin asks in his book *Mission in Christ's Way* if the evangelist is ready to be

I walked in thinking that I brought the gospel and the Spirit with me, but I discovered the good news was already being lived out.

changed by the encounter, or if he expects to change only the other person. I don't know if I was ready, but Don's life was changing me. He had found redemption, purpose, and a vision for who he was and how to give away his faith. I was witnessing a miracle; his freedom was uncertain, but he was transforming the prison that held him. I walked in thinking that I brought the gospel and the Spirit with me, but I discovered the good news was already being lived out. God's Spirit was moving, and God was lifting up Don in that forsaken place. My job was to bear witness to all God was already doing.

A few years ago, Don did get out of prison. He now owns a construction business that hires ex-cons. He has Bible studies at his home where he lives with his wife and two children. Recently, Don called me, overwhelmed by grief. The family living next door to him had lost their two sons in a drive-by shooting. Don had helped the young men when they had been released out of prison. Now he sat with their family as they mourned this horrible loss. He asked me what he should do; how he could help. I told him: "Suffer with them, cry with them, and you will suffer with Jesus. Let them tell you what they need, and let them teach you like you taught me. Let the event change you, like the prison visit changed me."

Who are the young people who live on our streets? They're tough, scared, broken, and tattooed. They are running from places that continue to haunt their present reality. They are courageous, bright, and resilient. They are like you and me. If we can move beyond all that makes them appear to be a problem to be solved, we will see them as children and young people, striving to make right their wounded pasts. The incredible truth is that they, with all their courage and faith, have much to teach us if we are willing to take the time to listen. This is the treasure that must not be buried and forgotten.

So he got up and went to his father.
But while he was still a long way off,
his father saw him and was filled with compassion for him;
he ran to his son, threw his arms around him and kissed him.
—LUKE 15:20

3

Every Prodigal Son Needs a Father

WHY DO SOME KIDS NAVIGATE SUCCESSFULLY THROUGH trauma and others don't? Why do some kids resiliently survive through years and years of abuse and others don't? Why do some youth survive life on the street and actually parent their children better than they were parented? Why do some youth pass their victimization on to the next generation and others don't? Why do some kids triumph over addiction while others fail? These are the million-dollar questions when working with street-involved young people.

I don't know why some kids are able to navigate through horrendous circumstances and abuse and some kids are not. However, I do know that kids who struggle desperately need relational connection. Every prodigal son needs a father. The "father" doesn't have to be genetically male or even related to the young person. But every youth who has run to the street to escape abuse at home needs someone to help him or her interpret the chaos of adolescence where unrecognized, unresolved, and uninterrupted trauma has existed.

In 2002, Michael Moore created *Bowling for Columbine*, a documentary about the Columbine High School massacre in Colorado. It focused on one of the most publicized stories of adolescent trauma and violence in US history. Two Columbine students opened fire on their fellow classmates, and then killed themselves. Moore interviewed Marilyn Manson, asking what he might have said, hypothetically, to the two young men who committed the murders. He said he would have said nothing. He only would have listened. Here is a musician that many of us would dismiss as being profoundly controversial and anything but moral, yet he spoke a profound truth. Manson's insight speaks to what young people in crisis need: safe places to run to and people who will listen. We cannot underestimate the power of listening.

Learning to Cope

New Horizons Ministries wanted to expand its programs to serve more effectively young women trapped in sex trafficking. These young women were involved in the sex industry at the height of the AIDS epidemic and during the rampage of the Green River Killer. Volunteers and staff members handed out surveys to the women asking them to rate in order of importance the services that would be most helpful to them. They had a variety of choices including medical assistance, drug treatment, housing, employment and education assistance, *and* someone to listen to them. The most frequently checked answer was "someone to listen to me." The women were regularly in need of medical help due to their vulnerability to sexually transmitted diseases as well as physical abuse. In the midst of all of this—the women still said they were looking for people to listen to them.

Not only do young people on the street need someone to listen to them, they also need someone to help them reclaim their identity. For many, the trauma and abuse they've experienced defines them—"I am what has been done to me." They have limited and impaired ability to see who they are in relationship to anything other than these horrifying events. Their minds, hearts, bodies, and souls are preoccupied by the abusive events that threaten to define them. They lose track of other defining characteristics that might serve to transform their identity.

I remember one young man called Dante who regularly came into our drop-in center. He smelled like he had defecated on himself. In the process of getting to know him, the staff members found out that he had lived in several group homes where he had experienced horrendous sexual abuse over an extended period of time. We wondered if his poor hygiene was a form of protection shaped by his past abuse. His spirit and his identity had truly been broken. In moments of rage, he would reel away and resist any touch. His violent outbreaks pushed everyone away. No one could touch Dante. No one could get close enough.

Getting to know him, the staff members found out that he had lived in several group homes where he had experienced horrendous sexual abuse.

In her book *Treating Abused Adolescents*, Eliana Gil provides abundant research findings on all the results, cognitive and other, from this type of trauma. The results manifest in a number of different ways. Children shut down their capacity to trust their own thoughts. The older the individual, the better they're able to cope with a traumatic event.

It seems rather obvious that children cope with trauma based on an accumulation of developmental assets. That is to say, a three-year-old will negotiate through a traumatic event with a 3-year-old's ability to reason, a 6-year-old will deal with an abusive event with all the developmental assets of a 6-year-old, and so on. The older a young person is when the trauma happens to them, the more development assets they have at their disposal to help them cope with the event. Most teenagers who end up on the streets are not coping with trauma as a 15-year-old young person, with 15-year-old coping mechanisms. They are coping with the trauma as the 15-month-old baby who originally experienced the abuse and trauma. At the time of the abuse their personality was defined by what was being done to them.

My wife, Linda, and I brought both of our children to work with us. As is the norm with most babies, oftentimes they would cry. My wife naturally responded by picking up the crying children. She assumed that they needed a diaper changed, to be fed, or simply to be held. Kids in the drop-in center who saw Linda pick up the baby cautioned, "You're spoiling them; you should let them cry." Linda always answered confidently, "No, I'm not spoiling them; I'm checking to see what they might be crying about. They might have a wet diaper or something might be hurting them. This is how I care for them as their mother."

One of the attributes of severely abused and neglected children is that they are very "happy" babies. They don't cry and they smile all the time. They have learned that crying gets them hit—and that smiling protects them. The kids who observed us parenting in the drop-in center—and associated responsible parenting with spoiling—were doing so based on the cues that they had picked up as infants or small children. They learned that when they cried they didn't deserve to be comforted, and that when they were uncomfortable or in pain adults were not going to do anything to relieve them.

Anchors and Rudders

James Garbarino, the author of *Lost Boys*, says that in order for young people to survive the insanity of trauma they need anchors—people who listen to them. I also believe they need "rudders"—people who guide and help them negotiate through the waters of adolescence. The likelihood of young people leaving the streets increases when there are "fathers," teachers, community groups, or churches to serve as anchors and rudders to help them navigate the chaos. Without anchors and rudders, young people have the potential of reliving their trauma over and over again.

Ages 2, 12, and 18 are the worst times for children to experience trauma. These are times of "natural" developmental separation with one's parents, guardian, or caregiver. Children and young people naturally separate from their parents and grow in developing their individual identity and independence. When trauma happens at these critical ages, identity development is severely crippled. The person feels isolated and alone rather than experiencing the growth of independence that leads to a healthy identity. Children and young people who experience abuse at these critical ages need a consistent caring community that will help them cope with these events.

Abuse and trauma shut down a person's capacity to trust his or her own thoughts. This fact is crucial to remember when working with abused kids. A young person who experiences violence day after day starts out realizing the actions are crazy, but as the craziness continues, they start to question their ability to assess the rationality or truth of their situation or environment. For example, when a young person is sexually abused, they think, *this is evil*, but as a parent or guardian continues to allow it to happen (or continues to be the perpetrator), the young person begins to question his or her capacity to distinguish right and wrong.

Only the strong survive. On the street, kids learn to take advantage of others. Trauma teaches them that they are either a victim or a perpetrator—these are their only choices. We can see why some young people go on to exploit and do damage to others on the street. They are seeking to protect their own identity.

Morally, youth traumatized by violence and victimized by abuse realize the disproportionate power perpetrators hold and view the victimized as powerless. These perceptions have significant impact on youths' concepts concerning God and omnipotence. A Christian home where sexual abuse is present causes a young person to struggle through enormous conflict as he or she attempts to wrestle with God being in control, yet unable to halt the horrible violation.

The parable of the prodigal son speaks to this need for a point of reference and a loving relationship (Luke 15:11–32). A boy asks for all of his inheritance and ventures far from family and home only to squander everything. His rebellious and narcissistic actions dismiss the importance of his family. Biblical scholars claim that he might as well have wished his father dead.

This young man drifts far from home and far from everything home represents. He becomes destitute in a foreign land with no family and no resources to help him. In order to survive he ends up taking a job feeding pigs. He becomes so hungry that he dreams of eating what the pigs enjoy. This young man's life spirals downward. He is isolated from his life with family and community, a first-century Jew working with defiled animals far from what's familiar. Desperate, he thinks back to the servants in his father's house. He realizes they're faring far better than he. Longing for the opportunity to be a servant in his father's household rather than a pig feeder, he runs home to beg for a job.

Not only is he welcomed when he returns, but he is celebrated as the one who was thought lost, possibly dead, and who now has returned home. The young man's father runs toward him with love and compassion, and embraces him with tears in his eyes. He celebrates the return of his son by giving the young man new clothes, a family ring, and an incredible feast.

The young man's older brother, who during this time has worked steadfastly for his father, questions the fairness of this welcome. Why does his younger, irresponsible brother deserve unmerited favor or unconditional love?

I want to make one thing clear before I continue. The focus of this parable is not a rebellious adolescent longing for independence. True, the young man is a symbol for an entire rebellious people who have squandered their lineage and legacy. However, the important point in the story of the prodigal son is God's pursuit of His children.

They're running from unsafe environments and abuse. God actively pursues and welcomes home the lost.

The kids I have known through my time at New Horizons are not on the streets out of rebellion. They're running from unsafe environments and abuse. God actively pursues and welcomes home the lost—this is how the parable relates to our young people who live on the streets.

I find the story crucial in discussing the role of identity and belonging in healing young people in the middle of trauma. Luke 15:17 reveals the young man in the middle of a pigpen, his inheritance squandered, starving to death. The verse states "he came to himself." It could be said that he finally recognized who he was. It was an incredible revelation during a time of crisis. He knew he didn't belong to the pigs in a distant land, forgotten and alone.

In remembering his father's house, he was able to grab hold of the fact that his identity was in his family and community. This family anchor held him even when he drifted a long way off. The tragedy in the lives of kids on the streets is they don't have a family and community to look back to as a point of reference for their identity. Once on the streets they're not dreaming fondly of the safety of their father's home.

A Place to Run To

At New Horizons, we have learned that kids in the middle of chaos and without a supportive community to surround them must have a surrogate community to foster the idea of a "home" to run back to. Kids on the street need adults to help them define their identity in new ways. The kids have taught me that any strategy to deliver services to them must be highly relational. *Programs don't save kids; relationships, connection, and community do.* So New Horizons seeks to affirm relationships that foster trust and build community and identity. Help is delivered in a highly relational context:

Volunteers and paid staff members go out on the streets, get to know kids, and then invite them into the drop-in center. Kids pick staff members to help them; very few are assigned an outreach volunteer or case manager. And these staff members are with kids throughout the program of care. A kid on the streets who meets someone from New Horizons will see the same person on the street, welcoming him or her for dinner at the drop-in center, visiting him or her in detention, or taking him or her to a movie.

Volunteers at New Horizons commit to a minimum one-year service; however, many outreach volunteers and staff members have been at New Horizons three, five, and ten years. Staff members who get to know street kids remain friends with the kids long after a commitment to New Horizons is over.

A friend once said, "Show me a kid who has seven mentors and I will show you a really messed-up kid." He meant that a revolving-mentorship system convinces kids that relationships are not consistent and cannot be counted on. We have found it important to work hard at creating relationships all along a youth's journey.

A friend once said, "Show me a kid who has seven mentors and I will show you a really messed-up kid."

We cannot be people who simply swoop in during a crisis. We must be there consistently so that when a crisis happens, we can be the family, the community, that the young person can reflect back on. To help kids in crisis we need to listen and extend a lifeline when things get hard.

Committed volunteers—screened, trained, and supervised—can be effective in serving homeless and street-involved young people, as professional counselors and social workers are also. By using trained volunteers, we move assistance from professional and programmatic to friendly, accessible, and relational. These volunteers build a unique, trusting friendship with kids.

Three times a year community members are invited to New Horizons Ministries training; this is the starting point of the deeply relational work of a New Horizons volunteer outreach worker. I believe volunteers become a point of reference for the kids and create a place where kids feel accepted. When the kids face a situation of overwhelming adversity, they can look back and realize that they have a friend, not because the person is paid, but because the person genuinely cares and wants to listen.

Many New Horizons volunteers go to court to support the kids when they are on trial. Although most of the volunteers have no previous knowledge or experience with the legal system, they teach the kids more by what they don't know, than what they do know. The young person watches a healthy adult negotiating through a complicated and unfamiliar system. The young person sees that a person doesn't have to have all the answers to negotiate through difficult circumstances.

➡ MIKE was a kid I knew well. He was an addict who had run away from home and a father whose expectations Mike felt he could never live up to. He didn't talk much about his dad, but from our conversations, I sensed that his father had been in the military and took his training very seriously. Mike said the way he made his bed in the morning had everything to do with how the rest of his day went. As he began to experiment with drugs, it was clear he was bringing shame on his family. According to his dad, Mike didn't need drug rehab; he just needed to "toughen up" and do things the right way. His dad had given him a choice about leaving home—stop using drugs or get out. Mike felt he had no choice but to leave. He knew he couldn't just "toughen up" and quit.

When Mike was sober, he was a delight to be around. He was articulate, polite, and hardworking. When he was using drugs, he wouldn't come around much. When I ran into him on the street, he would make the conversation short. I guess he thought when he was high he couldn't live up to my expectations either. Mike had lived in many foster homes, and one of his foster moms (Nancy) ended up volunteering at New Horizons.

When Mike turned 18, he signed up for a job-training program in another city. After a lot of discussion with Nancy, Mike moved in with Nancy and her husband for two weeks before leaving for the job-training program.

Nancy wanted to give Mike as much support as possible, so she stopped volunteering at New Horizons for those two weeks. New Horizons was committed to supporting this housing arrangement and assigned a counselor/case manager to support both Nancy and Mike. Mike stayed only a week before he ran.

With his departure, Nancy and her husband's stereo also disappeared. Three weeks went by with no word from Mike. Finally, I got a collect phone call from the King County Jail. Mike had been picked up on a car prowling charge. When I went to visit him the next day, he told me that he had run away from Nancy's house because it was just too much love all at once. During that visit, he didn't mention the stereo. The following week, when I visited Mike, he knew Nancy accused him of stealing the stereo. Mike emphatically denied it. He said, "I would never steal from Nancy or her husband. They were so kind to me. I left 'cause it was weird, but I wouldn't rip them off!" For the next few weeks, as I continued to visit him at the county jail, Mike talked about the stereo a lot. I always responded, "Mike, it doesn't matter if you did or didn't steal the stereo. I love you like a little brother. I don't visit you because you're innocent. I visit you because I care about you." It seems a little canned now, but I wanted him to know our friendship was not based on him being good or innocent. I was his friend regardless. After Mike did his time for the car prowl and was back on the street, he began attending Alcoholics Anonymous meetings and pursuing sobriety with a passion.

He never made it to job training, and after about two months of sobriety, Mike was back on the streets. He was working hard at staying sober, but without a place to stay, it was tough. We were eating dinner in a Chinese restaurant late one night, and I was going through a laundry list of all his accomplishments, trying to convince him that he had all the assets to make it away from the streets.

Suddenly, Mike blurted out, "I stole it! I stole the stereo! I am such a screwup! Why do you keep taking me out to eat and visiting me? I stole my Nancy's stereo!" Calmly, we talked about what he needed to do—apologize to Nancy and her husband. Mike thanked me again and again for helping him talk through the situation. I learned that day, like it or not, *I* was Mike's place to come back to.

By not focusing on Mike's innocence or guilt during our earlier visits, he was able to confess in his own time and then move on. If I had told him that I believed he was innocent, he might never have taken the opportunity to come back and revisit what he had done. I just needed to be a road sign of community. Nancy was amazing, loving, and truth-filled. When Mike offered an apology, Nancy and her husband firmly told him that he had violated their trust, but they were proud of his courageous confession. Mike was able to come to his right mind, and he knew he had a safe place that wouldn't let him off easy but would love him regardless.

➡ A couple of our staff members were on the streets late one night visiting with a kid, called **PIRATE**, who had been kicked out of the drop-in center for fighting. He was given the same message that all kids are given after they've been kicked out: "The bad news is that you're kicked out; the good news is that as soon as you leave we will set up a time to meet with you and figure out how you can get back in." Pirate was reflecting on the fact that he had been booted out of New Horizons' drop-in center, but had also missed several appointments with his staff member to discuss his re-entry. The staff members told Pirate that they missed him and that they were looking forward to him returning to drop-in. They encouraged him to take care of his business with the staff member who worked the night he was fighting. He shyly said he knew he needed to make the appointment and that he would be back in drop-in soon. "I know I broke the rules but I will be back because the staff members at New Horizons have a forgiveness policy. It's the rule above all other rules." Pirate knew he had a place to come back to, even when he had squandered several chances to meet with his staff member. He knew that New Horizons was a community that offered second chances.

⇒ New Horizons had an incredible father-and-daughter volunteer duo. SONJA is the president of a marketing consulting firm, and her father, DALE, is a very stoic, retired lawyer. He went through New Horizons' volunteer training about a year after his daughter. One night Sonja invited me and my wife and her mom and dad to come over to her house for dinner. Linda and I, Sonja and her husband, George, and Dale and his wife, Kris, laughed a lot about how much this retired attorney had learned from the kids. At one point in the meal, Sonja

Dale learned quickly that kids who have been beat up by the world protect themselves by being loud, arrogant, and cocky.

looked at her dad and said, "It really is amazing that you have connected with so many kids. I always wondered if the kids on the street would like you." Dale looked back at his daughter and responded slowly and thoughtfully, "Well, I didn't volunteer so that they would like me. I became a volunteer to tell them that I liked them!"

Dale nailed it. He loved a bunch of kids without expectation or ego. He learned very quickly that kids who have been beat up by the world protect themselves by being loud, arrogant, and cocky. Their survival on the streets is dependent on projected power and fearlessness. Dale didn't wait for the kids to accept and love him. In loving them first, he created a safe place for them to be themselves. Oftentimes we see street-involved youth reluctant to access programs or move toward caring resources in order to protect themselves from rejection and vulnerability. Kids need to be lovingly and gently pursued. Space needs to be created for them to discover their identity. This kind of selfless love brings kids back to New Horizons' drop-in center day after day. It brings them back in times of crisis, and when it is time to celebrate.

▶ A while ago, the intercom at New Horizons buzzed. I happened to be the one to answer it. I recognized the voice on the other end as that of EDGAR, a young man we had lost track of for a few months. I let him in, and we began catching up. He said, "I've been in jail, and I just got out. You guys are my first stop. I knew I could come back here."

A Place to Celebrate

Mike, Pirate, and Edgar all know they have a place to come back to and that their relationships with New Horizons are not based on innocence. Every time kids come in to drop-in they are celebrated—whether it's their birthday or they're just coming back in after being kicked out for an aggressive episode. Every time they are arrested, regardless of the crime, we visit them in jail. Young people know that they have a place to run to, a home. The drop-in center offers them a place to experience some clarity—to experience what it's like to be part of a community with a forgiveness policy.

The story of the prodigal son teaches us that in crisis people need consistent people to run back to. Kids on the street need a community that offers unconditional, positive regard and love. Christians must create—must be—

the "place" to run to, a community filled with forgiveness policies for those who are lost, hurting, and astray.

And the Word became flesh and lived among us,
and we have seen his glory,
the glory as of a father's only son,
full of grace and truth.
—JOHN 1:14 (NRSV)

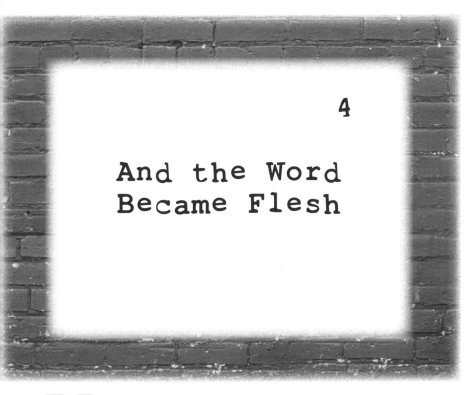

4

And the Word Became Flesh

YOUTH WHO ARE IN PRISON WRITE A LOT OF LETTERS to the staff at New Horizons. Rita Nussli, New Horizons' former executive director, received a letter from a young man, thanking her for all that New Horizons had done for him and ending with, "Thanks for showing me love with skin on it." Love with skin on it! Is there any better way to describe John 1:14? Jesus, God in our midst, becoming flesh for us. *The Message* states it this way, *"The Word became flesh and blood and moved into the neighborhood."* I love that translation, but I believe the young man who called us "love with skin on it" describes this passage better than any theologian. To truly hang out with kids—connecting with them where they are—is crucial to helping them move away from street activity. To connect in ways that exemplify love with skin on it is crucial in acting out the story of God in a way that can be understood by marginalized young people who have so few examples of Jesus among them.

God with Us

Whenever I think of Jesus being with me, I think of the church Christmas pageant when I was in fifth grade. Christmas pageants were always somewhat painful for me. Even back then I thought they did little to express "God with us"—what theologians call the incarnation. They were more a reminder that I had very little power and few connections in the small town where I grew up. I definitely had no clout with Dorothy Davis. She had directed a high school play once, so she became our church's pageant director. A self-proclaimed professional, she never did see my hidden potential.

The division of labor was the same almost every year. Sixth- and seventh-grade boys with even a shadow of facial hair got to be shepherds. They carried big sticks—a rod and staff. Unlike the rod and staff in Psalm 23, their rod and staffs were never any comfort. Shepherds got to whack kids who played sheep whenever they wanted to do so. Brian Davis, Dorothy's son, and two of his friends always played the wise men. Dorothy assured the rest of us that this decision had nothing to do with the fact that Brian was her son. It was because "he had a stoic look about him. You know we need stoic majestic magi," she would dramatically proclaim. I personally don't ever remember the Scripture claiming that the wise men were stoic. My fifth-grade year was especially tough. The pastor's son played Joseph, and the choir director's daughter played Mary. All the "little" kids were angelic beings draped in tinsel. That left the roles of farm animals for me and my no-good friends.

The sheep was the only animal without a heavy papier-mâché head. If you could avoid getting whacked by the shepherds, it wasn't such a bad role. However, you had to work your way up to that part. This year I was the donkey. I convinced my friend Billy Smith to join the fun. He never came to church, but a huge sack of candy given out the night of the production was enough of a bribe. Since I had recruited him, I got to be the head of the donkey and he got to be the backside. Wearing a papier-mâché donkey's head wasn't bad when I compared it to resting my head against the bottom of my buddy at each rehearsal. Billy made it to most of the practices and only occasionally socked me underneath the donkey costume. We were a team, and we were making the best out of a bad situation.

The glorious night of the pageant came, oh so quickly. I sat in the third-grade girls' Sunday School classroom, gray fabric around my legs, papier-mâché donkey head in my hand, and my greatest fear was about to be realized. It was 30 minutes before showtime, and Billy was nowhere to be found. He had bolted, and I was left alone. I would have to beg someone else to partner with me in the donkey costume. I couldn't lure anyone with the promise of a bag of candy; the truth was that everyone who participated in the pageant got a bag of candy. My only bargaining chip was to relinquish the head and become the backside.

Arthur Ditzler was a big sixth-grade boy. His close friends and his parents said he was big-boned. He came to the pageant to get his bag of candy and get out. I'll never forget his face when I pleaded with him to be the donkey with me. Dorothy Davis walked in, looking at me with dismay. I was a two-legged donkey with no butt and was about to ruin her pageant. You might be able to do the Christmas story without a cow in the barn, but you had to have a donkey, and I was all she had. The pageant was on the brink of disaster.

"Arthur, would you please be the donkey with me?" Arthur looked around me into the dressing room at the head that sat on the table. A heavy sigh reminded me of how alone and dependent I was at this moment.

Then he said, "Sure, I'll do it."

"You'll what?" I cried in shock.

"I'll do it, but I should be the back end. I'm way bigger than you." That night Arthur saved me, and I have been eternally grateful. He went about as far as a friend could go.

Many times, when I look back, I can laugh and cry about those lousy Christmas pageants, the vile shepherds, and arrogant wise men. But I also remember Arthur. His gracious act revealed to me as a kid the true meaning of the incarnation. He became the donkey with me and for me. He took the lousiest role of the Christmas pageant.

When I think about what Arthur did for me, I am reminded of how far God is willing to come to meet me. Those pageants didn't give me a positive image of baby Jesus wrapped in swaddling clothes; rather I saw Jesus being carried around by all the kids in the church who had political power and clout. The image I saw every year was Jesus held by the kids who counted for something. I was just a farm animal with no connection to the baby. Arthur came to me and became real love when he made his choice. Arthur, wherever you are, thanks for showing me love with skin on it!

Hanging Out on the Streets

Isn't this what God did when through Jesus He came close to humankind? By becoming flesh and blood, Jesus destroyed people's ideas and expectations of what God would look like, act like, and whom He would hang out with. Every time I think about the incarnation, I think about Arthur and how he made himself available to such a ridiculous task. He shared in my shame.

I have learned that if you're going to serve kids on the street, you have to go to some crazy places. You have to be on the street with the kids before they will access all the services that help them move away from the streets. Trust and relationship begins on the streets.

New Horizons sends teams of outreach workers to the streets almost every night to connect with the youth who are cautious about entering a drop-in center. Many kids have suffered such horrid abuse that they look at the world of ministries and social services with skepticism, and they see themselves as too far gone to be helped. For many young people, the streets are meeting economic needs, and they simply have no interest or time to visit a program. The streets are where the kids make their money, create contacts, and learn the hustle that helps them survive.

Outreach is acting out the story of Jesus coming close to us. It is a very practical way to meet kids on their own turf. For example, outreach workers set up a refreshment table and welcome young women who are prostituting. This is their only respite in the middle of a night with countless men. Outreach is not easy. Teams of two folks approaching groups of young people can be awkward, but it is the perfect way to extend the invitation—"If the streets aren't meeting your needs, if they aren't taking care of you, why don't you stop by the center?" Outreach workers try to honor the code of the street. They are not pushy; they just work to be a friendly, consistent presence.

Being with kids pushed to the streets can be scary. They're desperate, defensive, and have to keep up appearances.

Being with kids pushed to the streets can be scary. They're desperate, defensive, and have to keep up appearances. They don't have to talk to you; they don't have to respect you or be nice to you. This is their place, not yours. Jesus gave us the model: "The word became flesh and blood and moved into **our** neighborhood" (John 1:13 *The Message;* emphasis added).

Hanging out on the street with young people makes a person feel vulnerable. It can be scary, but it can pay big in relational dividends. Once you have earned the right to be with the kids, you've earned the right to go to some deep places with them. If you befriend a young man or young woman, you become a safe place for him or her to run to when times get tough.

A Brief Encounter

Back in the day, my friend Mick and I did a lot of outreach together. As a part of our routine, we often walked past the bus stops. Kids selling drugs and themselves use the bus stops as late-night hangouts. If they are questioned by police, they can simply say the bus hasn't arrived.

On a rainy night in February when Mick and I were out late doing outreach, we saw a young man sitting alone at the bus stop. We didn't want to walk up to a kid and say, "Hey, you look like you're prostituting!" Or, "Hey, are you homeless?" So we walked around the block a few times. When multiple buses flew by and the kid was still waiting there, we could pretty much bet something was happening.

➡ This particular night, the young man we noticed looked about 15 years old. He looked innocent, and scared, and like he had been on the street for about 38 seconds. Mick was smart. He asked the young man, "Hey, have you seen any kids that look like they're on the street? We run a drop-in center and would love it if you could let anyone you see know that they can stop by in the evenings." I thought it was a great approach, but the kid, IAN, didn't buy it. "What do you think I am?" he screamed at Mick. "I don't need social services involved in my business!" The way he said it let me know that he understood what it was like to have social services involved in his business. Ian was angry and wanted nothing to do with us. We apologized for bugging him, for making assumptions, and told him we hoped to see him again. That made him angrier. "You won't see me again!" he snapped.

In the weeks that followed, Mick ran into Ian countless times on outreach. Each time that Mick saw Ian, the young man got angrier and angrier. "What do you want?" Ian would exclaim in utter frustration. It became so bad that when Mick would see him, even from a distance, Ian would start screaming at him. Mick would consciously try to walk on the opposite side of the street from Ian to keep from upsetting him, but even then Ian would yell across the street, "I don't want a social worker; leave me alone!" Mick was a pretty smart outreach worker; it didn't take him long to realize that this kid didn't want our attention or our services. A few months passed, and like many kids, Ian sort of disappeared.

A Happy Coincidence

Mick was in San Francisco enjoying a much-needed vacation when he decided to visit another drop-in center for street kids. The drop-in center was built like a horseshoe. There was one entrance for administration offices and one entrance for the drop-in center. The two sections sat side by side like two storefronts, connected in the back by a kitchen and a bathroom. Mick was about to enter the drop-in center from the rear portion of the building when he looked up and saw Ian. Mick thought, *Yikes! How am I going to explain this?* He told the staff member about his tumultuous relationship with Ian, and they both agreed that in order to respect Ian's privacy that Mick would backtrack through the administrative offices and then leave out the front door. The drop-in door opened at the exact same time that Mick was leaving the administrative office. Mick and Ian ended up standing side by side—the concerned staff member looking on two steps behind. Mick immediately began to apologize. Ian looked surprised and asked if New Horizons did outreach in San Francisco too. Mick said, "Oh no. I was just getting a tour." Ian turned to the drop-in center staff person and began to describe New Horizons. He even told her that she should check out New Horizons if she was ever up in Seattle. He explained our services and told her all about the drop-in center he had never visited.

Who knows why Mick's presence on outreach created such an angry response from Ian. I'm glad Mick never decided that outreach wasn't worth it. I'm glad that Mick never decided that Ian was too far gone, even though Ian tried to convince him that he didn't need our help. I'm glad that Mick kept going out on the streets over and over again. What Mick did wasn't really all that profound. He just chose to continue to walk by the same kid, on the same corner, on the same night, week after week.

Whether the interaction is a one-time event or begins a life-long relationship with one of our young people, outreach is one of the best places to start with kids who feel like they've been thrown away. You meet them on their turf. You let them pace the interaction and the relationship. You make yourself vulnerable to the same streets they sleep on. In the end, as you go to them being flesh and blood, you stand as a physical reminder that they are not too far gone. You remind them that they are not forgotten, that they have a person or place to run back to in times of trouble.

The kids who live and survive on the streets need my friends Mick, Rita, and my childhood friend Arthur, or at least people a lot like them, to be love with skin on it. They don't need theories about the incarnation. They need real people to act out how far God is willing to go to let kids know how much they are loved. Love with skin on it—it is acted out. It's when we slip into a donkey costume, or when we go out looking for kids on rainy nights in February.

Someone to Care

We received a letter one day from a mother we had never met about a son no one could remember.

Dear New Horizons,

A few weeks ago my son was found dead. It's a long story, but to be brief, John struggled with addiction and mental-health issues. When we went to clean out his little studio apartment, we cried a lot and grieved the loss of our son. When we began to organize his few belongings, we kept coming up with New Horizons Ministries business cards. He had quite a few of them. They included phone numbers of staff and little notes describing your services. I don't know if my son ever came to your office. But I wanted to say thanks. It comforts me as a mother to know that when my son was out there and out of his mind, he had people like you reaching toward him. I rest in the fact that the cards remind me people cared and he wasn't all alone.

"Tell them, 'Israel crossed the Jordan on dry ground?'
For the LORD your God dried up the Jordan before you
until you had crossed over. The LORD Your God did to the
Jordan just what he had done to the Red Sea when he
dried it up before us until we had crossed over. He did this
so that all the peoples of the earth might know that the
hand of the LORD is powerful and so that you might always
fear the LORD your God."
—JOSHUA 4:22–24

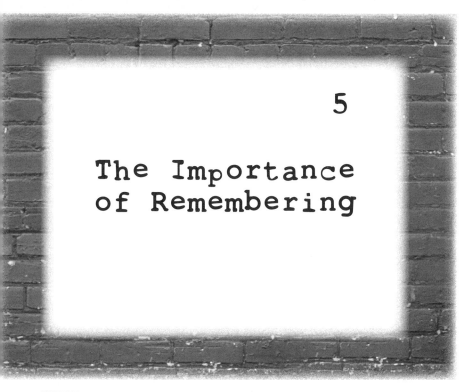

5

The Importance of Remembering

THE STORY OF THE CHILDREN OF ISRAEL CROSSING THE Jordan (Joshua 3:1 to 4:7) illustrates the importance of remembering our journey through life. Joshua got up in the morning and began to coordinate how to lead his people across the Jordan River, the last leg of their journey to the Promised Land. They were following the ark of the covenant—God's presence. The beautifully crafted box was a mobile presence that supported the Hebrew people through times of great transition. It went with the people as they moved into uncharted territory, territory filled with both promise and challenge.

Joshua received specific instructions from God on how to cross the Jordan River, and Joshua relayed these instructions to the Israelites. He instructed the people who carried the ark to move into the river and hold the ark in place as the people crossed through. After everyone crossed, all the people standing on the other side of the Jordan were instructed to stand still and observe as the people carrying the ark crossed over. After everyone had crossed the river safely, Joshua instructed them to build a memorial of stones to commemorate the historic crossing. He then told the people to bring their children to this place in the future in order to preserve the telling of the crossing and to celebrate God's great delivering power.

Reflecting on the Past

Music has an interesting power to take us back to the past and remind us of something or someone that we've temporarily forgotten. This is probably why as we get older our taste in music broadens. Rock and roll reminds me of my teenage years, hot summer nights, and a river that was the center of all of our activity. Jazz is creative and collaborative. It symbolizes people growing and creating spontaneously together. And hip-hop—well, I am a middle-aged Anglo man who loves hip-hop. It is a part of my community and my kids' culture. It reminds me of the sights and sounds of my neighborhood.

When my sons were young, we regularly went to our neighborhood high school's basketball games to watch the varsity basketball team dominate the schools from the suburbs. Nate Robinson, the five-foot-nine NBA dunk champ, got his beginning on the high school team. (If you are bored someday, research how many people who are currently playing in the NBA came from three high schools in South Seattle. Sorry, I pridefully digress.) Each game night, Nate's high school team would run out onto the court with the recording artist DMX blasting through the gymnasium speakers. "They don't know who we be," echoed across the gym. With all the stereotypes about inner-city schools, this song was an anthem of hope. With the fans primed and ready for a rousing game, a fan would shout out, "Show 'em where you come from!" and the game began. The concept of knowing where a person comes from and how history shapes a person's life blared from the speakers and the bleachers in this piece of urban poetry.

Young people who are able to begin the journey of exiting street life are the ones who are also able to begin the journey of remembering where they came from. They are able to remember their own pain in a raw and honest way. They are able to give voice to their own history and are able to declare the truth of its insanity. They begin to trust some of their own thoughts and are able to declare that the abuse that happened in their home or neighborhood was indeed crazy and wrong.

Dealing with Addiction

➡ DRUNK DOUG, as the other kids called him, was a young man on the street obsessed with drinking. He was drunk, belligerent, and physically busted up most days. He had such an alcohol problem that many kids on the street wouldn't hang out with him. You know you have addiction issues when other addicts don't want to be around you.

As well as struggling with an alcohol addiction, Doug also struggled with sexual addiction. He couldn't sit with me in a coffee shop without obsessing about the women who sat near us. His lack of impulse control increased by drunkenness made his addictions public and shameful. It was hard for us to be with him. He moved further and further away from the staff and kids at New Horizons.

He began to hang out with late-stage street alcoholics, commonly labeled *bums* and *winos*. They were the only group that could tolerate him. Doug was alone and slowly killing himself. At one point, we realized that we had not seen Doug for about six months. I wondered if he had left town or maybe died. I refused to call the medical examiner's office, afraid of what they might tell me.

One day I received a letter from Doug; the return address was NERF (Northend Rehabilitation Facility). He was in drug treatment, well, sort of. NERF was the alcohol and drug unit of the local county jail system. Doug had been arrested, and, since all his charges involved drunkenness, he had been sent to NERF rather than the downtown county jail. Men confined to NERF spend their days going to alcohol education, attending therapy groups, and watching drug awareness films. In the evenings other recovering addicts come to NERF to take part in Alcoholics Anonymous meetings.

In his letter Doug asked me to visit him. About a week later, I walked into NERF and found a new Doug. He looked great. He was a little heavy from three meals a day and a little manic from all the coffee, but he looked good, really good. "Ron, great to see you," he greeted me with excitement. He was ready to tell me his treatment story.

"I was at this meeting and I began to see how much damage my alcoholism had done to me and everyone around me," he said. "Everyone in the class had to make a list of our problems and describe how alcohol and drugs had been a part of them. Ron, I couldn't stop writing. I'm a mess. I have hurt people. I'm a drunk!"

He continued, "Ron, I went in the bathroom and looked in the mirror; I just looked at myself. I saw myself for the first time. Then God spoke to me. He told me that if I wanted to see myself, I couldn't drink. Drinking hides me from me and from anyone I get close to." Doug went from intense excitement to tears. "I hurt myself and women and friends. I might have to be here a while. I am really messed up."

A few months later when Doug got out of treatment, he stopped by to see me at New Horizons. He was hanging in there. He was sober and attending AA meetings. In his words, he was "trying real hard not to lust and to tell the truth about his addictions." He was once again very excited. This unbridled enthusiasm was his natural character trait when he was sober.

"Ron, did I tell you, God gave me what I always wanted?" I immediately became skeptical. I thought, *What health-and-wealth preacher had gotten to him?* But, curbing my desire to correct him, I just listened. "Ron, I got what I always wanted! The other day I was walking around Green Lake, and when I got about halfway around, I heard Jesus say to me, 'I'm walking with you!'" I must have looked a little puzzled; Doug read my facial expressions. "Don't you see, Ron? When I was a little boy I always wanted to go for a walk with my dad, but he was always drunk. Now Jesus is my Dad, and we walked around the whole lake together. Jesus told me that He was with me just like in treatment. I wasn't alone. He walked with me through treatment, and He walked with me around the lake. He's always been walking with me; I was just too drunk to realize it. Don't you see, Ron? I'm not alone. Jesus is with me!" Doug knew this was true. He was positively convinced. He didn't know a Bible verse, had never heard a sermon; he just plain knew it.

He was able to remember his pain and simultaneously experience God's ability to rebuild, restore, and redeem his life.

Drunk Doug now walks with Jesus. Not only was he able to remember the pain of his past, but he was also able to see God somewhere in the middle of all the chaos. He was able to remember his pain and simultaneously experience God's ability to rebuild, restore, and redeem his life. Doug has moved beyond the street. He is moving forward, going to AA meetings on his own, and befriending younger men who struggle with addiction.

The Crossing

Look back at Joshua 3:1–4:7. This biblical text is considered a piece of Deuteronomic history. Deuteronomic history is a genre of biblical literature that speaks of the way the Israelites understood themselves in relationship to God's ability to intervene in the middle of their chaos. Their history was not defined by a chronology of events, but rather by the action of God in the life of Israel.

I love this story of Joshua leading the Israelites across the Jordan. I think it has a lot to do with how kids who face their addictions and their painful family histories are able to move through these memories and recognize hope. They are all able to look back on their pain courageously. In Doug's case, he not only looked back courageously at the pain of his past, but he was able to see Jesus with him in the middle of his chaos.

Biblical scholar Robert Polzin points out the poetry in the crossing in *Moses and the Deuteronomist.* As the people cross the river, the ark stands still. It stabilizes the water for the people as they cross. When the ark crosses over, the people of God stand still. They try to take in all that this holy presence represents. The poetic nature of the passage is as the ark stands still, the people are able to move forward. As the ark moves, the people of God stand still in order to observe the movement of God.

I have seen this poetry lived out among young people like Doug. He was able to courageously stand still in the midst of the painful realities he experienced in treatment. Doug sat, waited, remembered, and faced himself in the mirror. Then he was able to move forward, knowing God was with him. When God moves we need to stop, listen, and discern. As God creates stability, it's time for us to cross the river and move into new territory. Both the moving forward and the waiting are done in the context of knowing God is present with us.

We live in a world filled with opportunities to cross rivers but many times we resist. When things are stable we sit back, relax, and enjoy the safety and security of the moment. We don't move forward. We also don't do a very good job of standing still in the middle of pain and difficulty. We want a pill, a book, or a counseling session that can fix it. We quickly attempt to move on, choosing to forget and to deny. It seems like we get it backward. We tend to move when we should stop and remember, and tend to sit back when God is behind us encouraging us to move forward.

The process followed by the ark and the Hebrews is exactly the opposite of our modern-day tendencies. The stability of God in the ark releases the Hebrew people to move toward the Promised Land. But the movement of God as the ark crosses the river is observed by a people who are willing to be still.

Joshua was a leader like Moses. According to Polzin, Joshua did more than declare the crossing; he used the event to train the people in the legacy of remembrance. He had the priest set up stones of remembrance and establish a place where the crossing is not only memorialized but theologized. God is remembered as being with them in the middle of their crossings. The stones now serve as a generational memorial to God being with the Israelites.

Seeing God's Provision

➡ I kept in touch with DAVID, the young man whose mother offered him acid for the first time when he was 12, throughout his adolescence and into adulthood. Through the years his life was filled with tragedy, one thing after another. His younger teenage brother was convicted of a bank robbery and tried as an adult. He was sent away to a maximum security prison when he was just 16. David's older sister died from alcohol poisoning. David's niece and nephew were sent to foster care after the death of their mother. They died six months later in a house fire. David's younger sister was murdered on the streets.

One time he shared a point of reflection with me. He told me about the night he returned home bleeding from a gunshot wound. He was terrified, and even though his home was chaotic, he went back seeking comfort in his panicked state. His mother gave him a tampon to stop the bleeding, but she wouldn't let him go to the hospital, because she knew the police would get involved. David said this was the most caring moment he could remember receiving in his home.

David's family was truly broken and he lived every day with the reality that his family had little capacity to care for him.

At another time, David and I talked about his incarceration. He was in a juvenile institution from age 16 until 19. He said, "I kind of liked it. I woke up every day and ate breakfast. I lifted weights and even went to school. The only bad part was my family never came to visit me, but other than that it wasn't that bad."

Many street kids manage pain through the use of illegal drugs. David was no different. He used heroin and drank a lot. In fact, David drank so much that by age 21 he looked 35. One day I got a phone call that David had overdosed on what doctors thought was heroin. He was in the hospital and in a coma. A few days passed as we waited to see what had become of David. Heroin overdoses can often leave people in a comatose state with severe brain damage.

David lay in the hospital a week before he woke up from the coma. When he did, he was unable to use his left arm, both his legs, and he had lost his ability to talk and communicate. A few weeks into his rehab David's speech slowly came back, but the paralysis continued. One day I sat in the hospital with David. The reality that he would spend the rest of his life bedridden or possibly, if he was very lucky, in a wheelchair began to sink in. We sat in silence together. I finally spoke, "I don't know how to say I'm sorry. It's going to be so hard. I'm sorry, David."

He thought for a while before saying, "Ron, I'm going to be okay. God is taking care of me. I took my legs and my arm away from myself. God spared my mind, my speech, and my one good arm."

Lying in a hospital bed, no family, never able to walk again, yet he reminded me that God was with him.

Somehow David was able to see God's provision even in the most tragic of circumstances. Walking through the shadow of death, David bore witness to the presence of God. I was overwhelmed by his ability to see God with him.

David's memory is a place of deep conviction for me. Lying in a hospital bed, no family, never able to walk again, yet he reminded me that God was with him. God spared him.

Defeat to Triumph

"Israel crossed over the Jordan here on dry ground... so that all the peoples of the earth might know that the hand of the LORD is powerful" (Joshua 4:22, 24). By placing the stones in the water, the Hebrews provided a way for future generations to know that God made a way where there was no way. Out of painful oppression and disorientation, God triumphed. He brought order to chaos and hope to the oppressed. God made something out of nothing.

In John 8, once again we see stones are a symbol of deliverance, a testament to the grace of God. Religious leaders set out to destroy an adulterous woman who had violated the law; however, Jesus halted the task when He knelt down and wrote in the sand. He challenged anyone without sin to cast the first stone. Stones of shame and accusation fell to the ground, and the men who held them walked away. Those stones sat in a pile and reminded the adulterous woman of her deliverance. Jesus transforms the memory of defeat to one of triumph by His intervention.

"Jesus answered, Even if I testify on my own behalf, my testimony is valid, for I know where I come from and where I am going, but you do not know where I come from or where I am going."
—JOHN 8:14 (NRSV)

6

I Know
Where
I Come From

KIDS ON THE STREET ARE NOT THE ONLY ONES WHO MUST look back and remember. Those of us who want to help young people work through traumatic events need to look back at our history and remember from where we have come.

Jesus made some bold statements. He referred to Himself as the light of the world, and He claimed that anyone who followed Him would never walk in darkness. He said that while the Pharisees were born from below, He was born from above. He told the Pharisees that they would all die in their sins if they didn't believe in Him.

The Pharisees are appalled that Jesus has the audacity to believe He can bear witness to Himself. They question how Jesus can speak with such authority about Himself. Jesus answered that He could bear witness to Himself because He knew where He came from, and He knew where He was going.

Knowing where you come from is crucial for anyone wishing to serve street-involved young people. It is the only way we can speak with authority. It begins to reveal where many of our values and beliefs were shaped by our own history.

The Ability to Relate

I attended the funeral of a young man who died in a car crash. He was new to the community, but he was already working two jobs to support his wife and two small children. The car accident happened late at night on a windy country road as he traveled from one job to the next.

➡ The young man was named KEVIN. He and his wife, Adrian, were friends of ours at the New Horizons' drop-in center. The couple had met on the streets. Kevin had no real family; he often said that he was the property of the State for as long as he could remember. Adrian was already a mother when she met Kevin. She was trying to parent her severely disabled daughter on the streets. The child's biological father was dying from complications due to AIDS and could not provide support for his former girlfriend or his daughter. So Adrian eventually lost custody of her baby.

Adrian was sickened, shamed, and grieved to have had her daughter taken away. She was dirty and lost, and scavenging food out of garbage cans on the street. She was haunted with guilt and regret. Regret that she had birthed a baby so sick and fragile. Guilt that she couldn't take care of her.

Adrian met Kevin shortly after losing her daughter. Theirs was a story of true love. They worked together to put their lives together, and they worked together to get Adrian's baby back. When the couple married, they were able to get custody of Adrian's daughter. Kevin did everything he could to parent this little child that was so sick and so dependent on him and his wife's love. He also worked hard to love his wife and give his new family the home neither of them had growing up. Their relationship was one that could be told in a storybook. Soon after they were married they had a son, and Kevin worked several jobs to make sure that they had all they needed and were financially safe and secure. The last time the staff at New Horizons saw Kevin was at Christmas party, just weeks before he died.

The young mother of two now struggled to arrange the burial of her husband. She didn't know anyone in the community where she and her husband had decided to start over. The preacher who officiated the funeral was a stranger. He read Scripture and recited his homily with the promise, "Jesus said He's going to prepare a place for you." He said, "In heaven there are many mansions," and then promised Adrian heaven and a chance to see her husband again. He went on to promise everyone a chance to know where they were going if they, too, were to die tragically in a car wreck.

The service lasted just about 30 minutes. When it was over, I walked through a rain-soaked parking lot to my car, wondering what had just happened. All those promises and proclamations, while they be true, did nothing for the little boy who played in a muddle puddle as I walked by. Kevin's son was wearing a black suit for a reason he could not understand. The promises of the pastor brought little comfort to a young mother who must now raise the little boy and his older sister by herself. *What went wrong*, I asked myself? The message was true. All that talk about heaven and assurance of life after death—I believe that. I have a master's degree and a doctorate in ministry, but as I drove away, the whole experience seemed cold, empty, and wrong.

I sat down a few days later and was thumbing through a little book by Henri Nouwen, *The Living Reminder.* "Forgetting the past is like turning our most intimate teacher against us"—Nouwen's words jumped out at me. "That's it!" I yelled. This was the answer I had been searching for, or at least part of the answer. In the middle of all that had transpired at the funeral and all that this poor young family had struggled with for some unknown reason, the pastor had not been able to relate to or identify with the myriad of painful emotions that filled the church on that day. The story of God was presented as some ethereal wish for a struggling and confused congregation who could not make sense of a true tragedy.

I grieve that the service—and the church at-large—is often too quick to offer "easy answers." The funeral did not provide us a time to feel, to grieve. No time to stop and acknowledge the doubt and confusion that comes with pain and suffering. It is gut-wrenching to lose someone too young, too early. My perception was that we had fallen victim to the easy answers in an effort to avoid the real pain. Yet the story of God is most profound when it comes in contact with the human story. This human story many times consists of no more than confusion, doubt, unbelief, and a desperate need for something more than we can understand. This is the beginning of our search for God.

Without a recognition of the feelings and thoughts that filled that room, the pastor's words sounded more like denial than faith. Not remembering his own pain, he couldn't communicate that Jesus is in the middle of those sorrowful places, during the painful moments, providing comfort and hope.

Personal Impact

So much of what street kids go through, while horrendous and evil, reminds us of the pain we experienced in our own lives. Listening to a kid talk about his pain will trigger our own tragic memories. Sometimes our effort to fix them is an attempt to remove the visible reminder that there is a lot of brokenness in the world—a reminder that alerts us to our own brokenness. The youth's tragedy becomes a project to redeem ourselves, to piece together the places in ourselves that are still broken. Maybe it was some of this that hindered the pastor in going to that place of feeling that day. Perhaps it was too close to his own pain; perhaps he is harboring something unrecognized and unaddressed. Perhaps his own unresolved pain served as invisible rudder steering him away from the very thought of how scary that funeral really was.

In order for young people to move away from damaging activities and lifestyles, they must have the courage to look back.

In order for young people to move away from damaging activities and lifestyles, they must have the courage to look back, to truly search out where they came from and discover how it impacts their present and their future.

Jesus says in John 8:14 that He knows where He comes from and this gives Him authority. I have come to realize that to be a healthy social worker, counselor, or urban ministry practitioner, a person has to be able to look back and know where he or she has come from. If we are going to authentically serve and love, we must do what we ask our kids to do—look back and truly remember. This means we must have a good understanding of how our history personally and corporately can impact our helping.

Jesus' response to the Pharisees is amazing. He commands authority. Who He is and how He is connected with

God is never in doubt. Throughout John's Gospel, Jesus speaks and acts with confidence. He does what He sees the Father doing. Jesus moves in unbridled power. His authority is not a secret in the Gospel of John like it is in Mark's Gospel where Jesus cautions people to not reveal the powerful nature of His healing works. In John 8, Jesus challenges those who tell Him that He can't make authoritative claims about Himself. His rebuttal to them is simple. He knows who He is, and this comes from knowing where He came from and where He is going. So I come back to this phrase from chapter six, "I know where I come from and where I am going."

This understanding of knowing who we are and where we're going is crucial to serving kids that come from tough places. This knowledge impacts who we are in the here and now. We know who we are by unwrapping our past, and we have faith in an unseen but certain future.

Looking Back

Many of us think we know where we come from. But I am talking about a memory that connects the then and there with the here and now.

➡ **I** grew up in a poor farming community. Most of the people who lived nearby were poor, hard working folks. One of my buddies growing up was a part of the wealthiest family on our block. His father was a janitor, and his mom worked at a local hardware store. They seemed rich to me. They were a two-parent, double-income, high-class family with lots of resources. That neighborhood taught me to be tough.

People in the surrounding area referred to the 200 or so houses in our little community as Taco Flats. It was a government housing project built for first-time home buyers in the 1970s. The name Taco Flats was spoken with a certain amount of scorn and disgust. So my friends and I lived our lives in reaction to that scorn. Every time we had to throw down with some other boys from the surrounding area, we would defend what little honor we had collectively.

What we didn't realize is that we were not defining ourselves, but we were allowing the opinion of people to mold how we interacted with the world outside Taco Flats. Our courage and our shame was a mere reflection of others' opinions of us. We were blind to the reality that their opinions defined our behavior and confirmed their racist and classist ideas.

When I was three years old, my dad died. My mom always had a tough time telling me who he was. She would say he was a good man—he never beat me. He wasn't a drunk. But she never really told me who he was, just who he wasn't. She did tell me, "When you're angry, Ronnie, you act just like your dad." For years I held onto my anger like a badge of honor. I was like the dad that I never knew. I was a skinny kid who had to be angry and talk tough. My bark had to compensate for my lack of bite. So anger became my friend. It ate me up and damaged my relationships, but for years I hung onto it. I had no idea that to give it up meant I gave up the one attribute I shared with my dad.

My mom was great. She only had a fourth-grade education, but she got a job at a nursing home and bought one of the "235" government-subsidized homes in Taco Flats. She supported us on $1.65 an hour. She was a lot older than all of my friends' moms. By the time we moved into the house, my sisters were married and raising their own kids. I was 8, and my sisters were 20, 25, and 26. They lived nearby, and they all helped parent me. I guess I had four moms. Mom worked a lot, and I was alone a lot. I was stuck somewhere between raising myself and having way too many moms too much of the time. Mom, sometimes overwhelmed with being a single parent, would say as a default mechanism for discipline, "You're lucky your dad isn't here." Or, "If your dad was here, you wouldn't do that."

Too many moms, too much time alone. I struggled with a paradox about my dad. I had both an intense longing to be with him but resented what he might have been like if he had been alive or had been there for me. Sometimes I found myself wishing I knew him and sometimes I felt relieved that he was gone. Until I figured out how my past had had an impact on me, I had no idea why I felt that way.

Nouwen says that turning our back on our past is like turning our back on our most intimate teacher. I thought I knew where I came from because I was down with my hood and defended my boys even when they were flat out wrong. I could get mad, scare others, and the anger made me look powerful. No women were going to tell me what to do. I didn't need another mother. I had a few, and a few were too many.

But those things that I did not remember, or better said, those things that I did not understand from my past had control of me. I would go to a wedding and not line up for the best of buffets. It brought back the humiliation of waiting in the food bank lines with my mom. It reminded me of the charity Christmas baskets we received. My anger was out of control. Little things that to most people are unimportant impacted me in a huge way. My anger was unpredictable because something boiled beneath the surface that activated me, and I had no idea where it came from.

Somewhere between not having a dad, being angry, and being a lonely little boy with too many moms, I was blinded to the real me. I was emotionally unaware. I had no idea of my impact on the men and women who crossed me. I was lonely, hurt, scared, and emotionally dangerous. I was a Christian in ministry watching street kids who were stuck in old behaviors too. However, I watched many of them courageously look back at their pasts, make choices to walk away from their tragic histories, and move forward into hope-filled futures. Many times the difference in those kids who were able to move forward and those who were unable to do this was the young person's willingness and maturity to look back. I had to muster up the same courage. So I began to ask questions about myself and my impact on others. I listened as those who cared for me told me the truth about myself. I began to have conversations that led me to discover my current reality is a reaction to a past I had not really remembered. I had never stood still long enough to take inventory of how my hurt and unremembered pain was rearing its head in how I served, how I loved, and how I lived with others.

I didn't realize that my current reality is not about current events; rather it is all mixed up with the past.

You see, when you don't know where you come from, the past and the present find a way of merging. I didn't realize that my current reality is not about current events; rather it is all mixed up with the past. Every interaction, every conflict, was me reacting in the dark, turning my back on my past, and my past bleeding out onto everything in the present. Many conflicts became horribly overblown, because I was still acting like a little boy defending my honor. I was comfortable with anger, but I could not identify less powerful primary emotions that sat under the surface. Many women unconsciously reminded me of my older sisters trying to parent me. Many men reminded me of the fear that had engulfed my memories about what my dad might have been like if he would have lived. I learned that I had to honestly investigate and deal with my past before I could present for my wife, my children, and the kids I served.

Moving Forward

This act of remembering is not only necessary for an individual's emotional and psychological awareness, but it's also important for us as a society. Sociologically, in order for us to address the deep wounds in our communities, we must realize where we are as a nation and where we have come from. We need to explore social location, distribution of power, and how serving others is perceived by those being served. For example, who am I as an Anglo heterosexual man, and how does this social location impact how I read the Scripture and interact with my world?

Most days I ride the number 7 metro bus to work. The number 7 isn't just an arbitrary bus route; it serves the most diverse community in Seattle. The number 7 runs through the University District, into downtown, and through the poorest sections and the most ethnically diverse sections of the city. The local number 7 is the primary source of transportation for most of the folks who ride it. Sometimes I avoid the 7, and take an express bus to downtown. I have a love/hate relationship with the number 7. At night it drags people home from who knows where, and for those who have no home it serves as shelter for two bucks. Whether I love it or hate it, I have to confess it's always been a great teacher.

➡ One night in particular, it was too late to catch an express, so I rode home on the local number 7. I sat across from a really drunk woman and **ADAM**, a kid I had coached in little league. Adam and I hadn't seen each other in a couple of years, so we were catching up. As we talked, the woman carried on her own conversation with everyone within three aisles of her seat. She took time to ask me how Adam and I knew each other. I told her that I was his baseball coach a few years back. I went on to tell her that he was a good boy, and it was great to see him again. The woman looked at me for a long time then carefully and quietly asked me if she could tell me something. Of course, I told her I was willing to listen. She had a kind and maternal look on her face as she began to teach me. "He's black, and I am black. You look like a nice enough white guy, but…" She hesitated, choosing her words like someone far more sober. "You shouldn't call him a boy; he's a young man. Too many white men have used that word *boy* for too long." As soon as she said it, she began to apologize to me. She said she meant no harm. I interrupted her and thanked her. She kept apologizing, and I kept telling her how grateful I was that she had sat between Adam and me. I thanked her again for telling me the truth that I had been blind to see. She got off the bus apologizing, and I thanked her again.

The drunk lady and the number 7 made me realize that a term like *boy* is inappropriate considering our shared history. What it meant in the past has everything to do with what it means now. I, as an Anglo man, had no idea the power and the baggage I brought into every relationship I stepped into. I began to think about the kids I had relationships with on the streets and at New Horizons. I wanted to apologize to many of them. I wanted to ask them if they could honestly tell me how my culture and gender had had an impact on our conversations. The drunken woman on the bus had told me the truth. I had never thought about it before, but it was the truth. I wanted to live in the truth, and I wanted my co-workers at New Horizons to live in the truth.

Jim Wallis, in his memoir *Faith Works,* says, "Building a nation on land stolen from indigenous people, with the use of slave labor from kidnapped black Africans, has left us with a legacy we have yet to fully deal with. The lack of true repentance for that sin still confounds our efforts to overcome it."

We live in a culture of discord even today. Wallis wrote a decade ago, "Diversity is widely perceived as a cause for conflict more than for celebration. The question is: why?" I believe that many of us, as a community, really don't know where we come from. We don't realize that many of the people we interact with have never really looked at our nation's history. Some of our ancestors were pulled here by opportunity, others pushed by tragic circumstances in other nations, and others were kidnapped. As our borders pushed south and west, hundreds of Latin Americans and the People—Native Americans—were displaced in the name of Manifest Destiny.

Eric Law, a gifted conference leader and author of *The Wolf Shall Dwell with the Lamb: A Spirituality for Leadership in a Multicultural Community*, is an expert on the problem of "isms" in America. When he spoke to the staff at New Horizons Ministries, he called reconciliation "iceberg work." Law says that most of our collisions across gender, racial, ethnic, and cultural lines happen like icebergs colliding below the surface. We tend to focus on the stuff we see above the water line and ignore the dangers that lurk below the surface. Law encourages communities to go deeper, below the water line, exploring not just what we see, hear, and feel but the values, beliefs, and truisms that motivate our actions and dictate lifestyle choices.

Both Wallis and Law would challenge us to dig below the surface, exploring the impact of what we don't see on how we live our lives. The then and there of our personal lives and of our national history must be uncovered if we are to move ahead.

If we dig into the hidden portion of the iceberg, if we know where we come from, then we can help people who sit at the margins created by our collective past. Jesus knew where He came from. He was completely present. He did not allow His past to become a hidden force merging into His present interaction.

The writer of 1 John speaks to this principle when he says, *"If we say that we have no sin, we deceive ourselves, and the truth is not in us. If we confess our sins, He who is faithful and just will forgive us our sins and cleanse us from all unrighteousness"* (1 John 1:8–9). Sin is simply all that separates us from being who we were created to be. We are called to recognize how we, through our brokenness, have created mechanisms to protect ourselves and to heal ourselves. However, because these mechanisms are born out of our own hurt, they are birthed in darkness. They damage those around us and further separate us from the light that illuminates our pain in a way that we are truly healed. Remembering our past and knowing how it impacts our here and now is a flashlight that exposes the motivation behind our actions and truly sets us free from forgotten forces that lead us.

Having a sense of our past gives us the freedom and confidence to move forward in the unseen plan of God.

Jesus knew where He came from, and He was confident in where He would end up. The Pharisees had no control over Him. He didn't need to get caught up in their games for power and control. His interactions were never about an unresolved past. He had spiritual eyes to see the physical and spiritual reality of every conversation He was in. He knew who He was. The "end" of the story in Revelation is that of Jesus being victorious. Jesus wins. Having a sense of our past gives us the freedom and confidence to move forward in the unseen plan of God. Knowledge protects us from being manipulated by the forces that truly have no power over us. If we know our past and we are confident about our future, we can be completely present in the moment.

First John 1:8–9 challenges each of us to have the courage to ask: Where have I come from? How has my past impacted me? Does my present get mixed up with stuff from my history that I don't understand? Do I have the courage to admit where I came from and to ask God to shine a light on how it impacts my behavior now? I pray that we would also have the faith and confidence to know where we are going, to discern our spiritual destiny, to believe that Jesus wins in the end, and to rest in the knowledge that we do not have to fight our own battles. If we search out where we came from and identify where we are going, we will be empowered to move forward and relate to the people we are trying to help.

*"I have not come to call the righteous,
but sinners to repentance."*
—LUKE 5:32

7

Dinner at New Horizons' Community Table

HUNGRY KIDS ON THE STREETS OF SEATTLE CAN GO to New Horizons for breakfast and dinner. The center has always served food. At first it was fried bologna sandwiches, but for more than 20 years now, the kids have been offered incredible meals. While a clothing room, laundry facilities, and access to showers meet kids' essential needs, breakfast and dinner are the centerpieces of activity.

Food groups are formed by local businesses, churches, and small groups. They each make a six-month commitment to serve one meal a month. The groups purchase, prepare, and serve wonderful, nutritious, home-cooked meals. Many of our groups have a "signature" dish that they serve.

- The food group from Rolling Bay Presbyterian Church is famous for their cheesy shrimp and grits; breakfast pork chops smothered in gravy; stuffed croissants; and fried eggs to order.

- Cross Sound Presbyterian Church serves breakfast burritos smothered with cheese; fresh guacamole and homemade salsa; plus a fresh fruit salad; yogurt; and breakfast bars. All of the meals are prepared with love and care.

These meals at New Horizons Ministries fulfill a multitude of purposes. The most obvious is that they feed hungry kids. Without meal services provided by ministries and social service agencies, the homeless kids would "dumpster-dive" (search for food in garbage cans), "dine-and-dash" (order and eat at a restaurant and then run out without paying), "spange" (beg for money or food), or simply go without eating.

The volunteer food groups also serve as a way to introduce people to the work of New Horizons in a very natural, practical, and nonvoyeuristic way.

- Nearly 150 food group volunteers (about 35 groups) come to New Horizons each year to help feed the hungry kids.
- These volunteers work with the one staff-hospitality coordinator to provide more than 11,000 meals, so they are helping New Horizons to stretch the payroll dollars too.

Another important purpose the food group volunteers fulfill is to allow more time for outreach volunteers and staff to interact with the kids at mealtime. They're able to focus on building relationships, rather than trying to frantically put together a meal for 50 kids with random donations.

- So, on any given night or morning if you were to stop by New Horizons' drop-in center, you would see 6 or 7 food service volunteers unpacking bags of groceries, laughing, and getting ready to prepare a meal for 50 to 75 hungry teens.

- One food group volunteer from Union Church describes what he does this way: "We start with a shrimp cocktail and serve a marinated chicken breast, garlic mashed potatoes, and fresh green beans. We will have brownies and vanilla bean ice cream for dessert. I tell our church, if I could, I would have all these kids to my house for dinner, but because my table isn't big enough I have to serve them here. I want them to be served the way I would serve any guest at my own table."

Free Lunch

Over the past few years I have been learning about the philosophical and theological implications of food. Food goes a long way in fulfilling our mission at New Horizons Ministries. It puts the staff at tables getting to know kids, connects the church with homeless kids in a very tangible way, and feeds hungry kids. All of this should convince me that programs to serve food to the needy are a good idea. But to be honest, words like *food bank, mission, free food, food stamps* all send me back to my childhood.

➡ I remember images of mean lunch ladies giving me my "free" lunch while looking down their noses at me because I chose chocolate milk over plain milk. I knew the look. They glared at me as if to say, "You don't deserve the luxury of chocolate milk." As an eight-year-old I couldn't understand why chocolate milk was worth so much more than plain milk, and I also didn't understand why I didn't deserve it.

Along with the glorious annual Christmas pageants that my church put on every year they also had a Christmas ritual of caroling and delivering Christmas food baskets to families in need. I remember hearing the announcement on Sunday mornings. "It's that time of year when we give to the widows and orphans," the pastor would declare. "We are going to meet at the church, carol around some neighborhoods, and hand out food baskets to the poor. It sounded fun. But my mom worked most Sundays—and caroling wasn't something she was interested in doing. I forgot all about the opportunity to carol with my church until one random night when both my mother and I were watching television and heard singing outside our house. We followed the sound to our door. When we opened it there were the members of our church singing Christmas carols. We could not sing along because we didn't make it to the door fast enough, and who knows the second verse to any Christmas carol.

Someone in the group wished us a Merry Christmas and handed us a basket. The basket was filled with summer sausage, cookies, crackers, and one of those horrible fruit cakes. It was at that moment that I felt far away from the group of people that made up my mother's church. I realized in a flash that my mother and I were the widows and orphans that the pastor had talked about at church. I never thought of myself in that way. We were "the poor." As the carolers walked away from our house spreading Christmas cheer, I remember thinking, *I could have lived without the food basket, but it would have been nice to have been invited caroling.* I had never realized that I was poor until that night. I didn't know I was part of a category of people who needed help.

My mother, who raised me by herself, did everything she could to keep me away from free-food handouts and shame-filled food bank lines. But I remember them. They were lines that led to canned meat, pounds and pounds of cherry tomatoes, and huge blocks of cheese too big to be carried by my scrawny, preadolescent arms. I'm still a little hesitant when it comes to lines that involve food. No matter how nice the buffet, I would rather wait than line up, and a continental breakfast—yikes—no matter how nice the hotel, I avoid those lines like the plague! I guess when I was a child I learned that food was never free. I learned that food marginalizes and separates people. It says who has power and who does not.

I have other memories of food growing up. One of the most vivid is of my mother's fried chicken. My wife, Linda, says that I shouldn't even ask her to try and compete. I will never forget, after church services that were way too long, coming home to my mom's fried chicken. Anyone and everyone was welcome on those rare Sundays when my

I learned that food can go a long way toward welcoming people and just making them feel plain good.

mom didn't have to work. People would try to be polite, while simultaneously jockeying for a place at the table that would entitle them to the piece of chicken of their choice. Those were the days when I learned that food can go a long way toward welcoming people and just making them feel plain good.

Rubbing Elbows

Every kind of kid drifts though the doors of the New Horizons' drop-in center. I have had to get pretty creative in striking up a conversation with some of them. It's not unusual to have a kid walk in, flop down on the couch, and respond to the question, "Is there anything you would like to work on?" with "Yeah, I would like to be a brain surgeon." Realizing that many youth have a difficult time connecting their present situation with a future goal I say,

"Well, most brain surgeons I know have a GED; maybe we could start there." Even with glorious food and tables of fellowship, conversation is sometimes challenging. What do you talk about with a kid just off the street? You can't ask 20 questions; that's not a conversation, it is an interrogation. You can't ask closed-ended questions, because then a kid will answer yes or no until you leave them alone. I have found the best place to start is letting them teach me. I ask kids who their favorite band is, or their theory on religion, or their favorite food and how to prepare it. Kids love to give their opinion and to teach if they are invited to do so.

➡ One particular evening I noticed A YOUNG MAN sitting alone at a table in our drop-in center. I went over and began a conversation with him. He told me his parents were first-generation Americans from Ethiopia and that they didn't understand him anymore. I turned the conversation to food and asked if there was a good Ethiopian restaurant in Seattle. He told me of a little place near where I live. When I assured him I would try it, he cautioned me, "It's very traditional; we all eat from the same bowl." I let him know I was familiar with the custom, but he once again cautioned me. He shook his head as if to say that I really didn't understand what I was saying yes to. He held out his dirty hands and asked, "Would you share a bowl with these hands?" Suddenly the story of Levi rushed to the front of my mind. That was the ministry of Jesus.

Jesus always seemed to be eating at people's homes. It is interesting to read the accounts of these dinners. Luke's Gospel puts Jesus at the table of many people (5:27–31; 7:36–50; 10:38–41; 14:1–23; 19:1–9). When Jesus eats at the house of a tax collector or a woman or any person categorized as a sinner, He ends up having a wonderful time. But put Him at the table of a religious leader or the social elite, and the dinner disintegrates into one of those holidays you could spend carving turkey with relatives you don't really like.

One of my favorite stories is Jesus at the house of Levi (later called Matthew) in Luke chapter 5.

After this he went out and saw a tax collector named Levi, sitting at the tax booth; and he said to him, "Follow me." And he got up and left everything and followed him. Then Levi gave a great banquet for him at his house; and there was a large crowd of tax collectors and others sitting at the table with them. The Pharisees and their scribes were complaining to his disciples, saying, "Why do you eat and drink with tax collectors and sinners?" Jesus answered, "Those who are well have no need of a physician, but those who are sick; I have come to call not the righteous but sinners to repentance" (Luke 5:27–32).

Jesus was invited to the house of Levi, a tax collector, where Levi had prepared a large banquet in Jesus' honor. Levi did what anyone would do; he invited his friends to dine with his new friend, Jesus. The spiritual men of Jesus' day were repulsed that Jesus would choose to associate with a tax collector, much less participate in one of his functions. They questioned the idea Jesus could be sent from God and yet eat and drink with tax collectors and sinners. They believed that if Jesus was the holy one sent from God, He wouldn't rub elbows with the dirty and defiled in His community. He must be separate, bearing witness to the separateness of God.

The Pharisees have only part of the story correct. They were men who were set apart and did everything humanly possible to protect the law. In many ways they represented the transcendence of God. God is set apart, different from humans. Jesus sitting at the table with tax collectors was beyond the Pharisees understanding. How can Jesus' claim to be God, exemplify His transcendence, while at the same time eat with such people? In eating with Levi, Jesus revealed the whole story.

People in Jesus' culture used food to distinguish people who had power and social status from those who did not. Who you ate with said who you were, socially and economically. The Pharisees saw God as separate, exclusive, set apart; however, Jesus associated with people who were pushed away pushed out and forced to live on the margins. Jesus demonstrated that God's transcendence was not for the sake of exclusion but to extend mercy and healing. Jesus sat with the people that God loved and exemplified God's imminence and desire to be in relationship with humankind.

In the first two chapters of Genesis, we see two examples of God's creative power. Genesis 1 shows the transcendent nature of God. God spoke into existence the world. He separated light from dark and land from water with His word. God spoke and creative activity happened.

In Genesis 2, God bent down and formed humankind with His own hands. He is the Creator—a gardener and a potter. God was physically involved in creating humankind. God shared His very own breath with humankind. God's action of breathing into the lungs of humanity was as intimate as a kiss. God kissed us into existence. In Genesis 2 we see the part of God that the Pharisees had missed. God is all-loving; He rolled up His sleeves and formed humankind with His hands—He gave His own breath to His creation. God is truly different from man. The Pharisees understood this, but in their effort to be holy they had missed a few important elements to the story: (1) God's desire to be in relationship with people; (2) The Pharisees needed a doctor as much as the tax collectors; and (3) God is willing to associate with anyone who invites Him in.

The link between the call of Levi and Genesis 1–2 was first shared with me in a sermon at Calvary Chapel in Seattle by Dr. Blaine Charette, and it was further illuminated by a young man from Ethiopia, whom I never saw again. I am indebted to Blaine, a professor of New Testament, and to a teenager I will only see again in the next kingdom.

What happened at Levi's house? Mealtime, which had been an exclusive ritual that mediated social relationships, became an inclusive relationship-building event. Today, when we use food to welcome and include, we are putting into practice deep theology. We are telling the story of Levi, Mary, Martha, and Zacchaeus. We sit at a table and welcome people into something much bigger than dinner. We begin new relationships, rekindle old friendships, and act out the story of God in the shape of hospitality.

I am indebted to Blaine, a professor of New Testament, and to a teenager I will only see again in the next kingdom.

Gifts of solidarity and hospitality have little to do with food baskets and mean lunch ladies, but everything to do with what happened at my mom's table. Building relationships and community are manifested every time volunteers and staff at New Horizons sit and share a meal with a young person from the streets. This is what I learned at the table of my Ethiopian brother. He was not only welcomed at the table but for a moment we were able to switch places. We shared only one meal, but he knew the context of the meals described in Luke, and he became my teacher.

We can use food in a magical way. The same way my mom used her fried chicken on Sundays, the same way

Jesus used a dinner invitation, the staff and volunteers of New Horizons use food and hospitality to welcome kids back into community and relationship.

As Jesus was getting into the boat, the man who had been demon-possessed begged to go with him. Jesus did not let him, but said, "Go home to your family and tell them how much the Lord has done for you, and how he has had mercy on you." So the man went away and began to tell in the Decapolis how much Jesus had done for him. And all the people were amazed.
—MARK 5:18–20

8

Refusing to Believe the Voice of the Crowd

THEY WENT ACROSS THE LAKE TO THE REGION OF THE Gerasenes. When Jesus got out of the boat, a man with an evil spirit came from the tombs to meet him. This man lived in the tombs, and no one could bind him any more, not even with a chain. For he had often been chained hand and foot, but he tore the chains apart and broke the irons on his feet. No one was strong enough to subdue him. Night and day among the tombs and in the hills he would cry out and cut himself with stones.

➡ When I first started working with kids on the street, I walked through Blood Alley every day. Apparently lots of craziness happened there, and the kids gave it a name to serve as a warning. Blood Alley was located directly behind our drop-in center. Each day, whether I wanted to or not, I visited the alley to empty the garbage and clean the back stairs. On the wall adjacent to the back steps was graffiti in big red letters—**Don't you know your all ready DEAD!** (I guess spelling was not the point.)

I always thought this was a tragic declaration. The graffiti served as a prophetic voice that reminded kids of the inevitable outcome of street life. It communicated to all who read it that it was simply too late. It was too late for the kids who shot dope, too late for those who prostituted, too late for all of the kids on the street. The big, bold words hopelessly stated that they were all too far-gone.

Sadly this was more than just a spray painted message on an alley wall. This statement is a mainstream attitude about young persons caught in addiction and involved in street activity. I get asked all the time: "How many do you really get off the streets?" "What do kids look like when they're successful off the street?" "Shouldn't you spend your time with young people who have a better chance to succeed?" Is it simply too late for kids who are incarcerated, who are addicted, who are infected with HIV, or who sell themselves to survive on the street?

That alley and the graffiti remind me of the story of the demon-possessed man in Mark's Gospel. When I read the story of the demoniac, I think of a young man pushed to the margins of his community. I hear the echo of the red letters—*Don't you know your all ready DEAD!*

Defying Oppression, Torment, and Fear

In binding the demoniac in the cemetery, the community resigned itself to the idea that the man was already dead, that he was too far-gone to help. They thought his life was not salvageable. The man was so sick that he was beyond the community's ability to fix.

The community that at one time knew his family, went to synagogue with him, and worked with his father now have him put in chains in a cemetery. Of course, all of this could be a stretch. However, we do know this. For some reason the community had taken a man who once lived among them and bound him in a place for the dead. The story goes something like this:

A crazed man possessed by demons, subdued by no one, ran toward Jesus and begged for release. The demons, which had the power of a Roman legion of soldiers, begged Jesus to leave them alone. If they were to be driven out of the man they asked to be cast into a herd of swine. Jesus granted the demons' request. At that point the pigs, either out their pig minds or completely in tune with the power of evil, chose to end their own torment with a mass suicide. The man, once out of control and befriended by only the dead buried in the cemetery, now sat lucid. He wore the clothing that he had abandoned long ago. Then, those who heard the remarkable story, or witnessed it firsthand, asked Jesus to leave. The crowd was as anxious about Jesus' presence as they were about the presence of the former demoniac living in their community.

At the end of the story, when Jesus left the town, He didn't take the man with Him. He only asked the man to bear witness among his people to the mercy of God. This story is different from others in Mark's Gospel where Jesus told the people He healed to tell no one. In the story of the demoniac, Jesus requested that the man bear witness to a community that had once bound him in the tombs.

Look at this story more closely. The demon had power over all the methods the community used to subdue the man. The chains could have been easily broken by the demon possessed man, and no one in the community would have been strong enough to subdue him. After Jesus' miraculous work, the crowd begged Him to leave. The crowd who was powerless to control the demon requested the deliverer to leave.

Perhaps the man who sat with the dead in a cemetery, a safe distance from the living, reminded them of their inability to fix the brokenness in their world. Is the crowd trying to bind the demons, or do they just want to remove the man from their sight? Out of sight, out of mind, in a cemetery bound and restricted, so he can no longer remind them that some things are out of their control. It is interesting that all of the characters in the story, except for Jesus, are plagued with oppression, torment, and fear. A tormented man cut and bruised himself to stop the haunting demons from torturing him. The demons begged Jesus not to torment them. The crowd who wanted to subdue the chained man appears to fear the power of Jesus as much as the power of the demonic force. Even the pigs are tormented and chose death over demonic possession. Jesus stood in defiance of oppression, torment, and fear.

Mark's Gospel emphasizes the community's inability to bind the demon-possessed man. The crowd was not able to subdue the man or control him. "Did they attempt to subdue the demon or did they attempt to subdue the man?" The tormented man cut himself in an attempt to control his circumstances, and to release himself from the demonic force within his body.

This man had been pushed to the edge of his community, to the margins of a cemetery to be cared for by the dead. Did the crowd believe the man was too far-gone, or "already dead"? If the man was condemned to a cemetery he was out of sight. He was no longer a visual reminder of the community's inability to fix a hopelessly uncontrollable member of their town. As long as he remained among them, he stood as a physical reminder of the brokenness in their world— brokenness they were powerless to fix.

Not Too Far-gone

This story struck me because of where I live and what I have done for a living for the last 25 years. I have served kids labeled as uncontrollable, demon possessed, and too far-gone by the community. These kids ran away from home or were thrown away by the social service system, and were adopted by the culture of the streets.

➡ In some small way **I** was thrown away too. I remember when my high school music teacher called me "Ronnie the reptile." This Christian teacher told me that I earned my name by sliding into and out of his class every day. My psychology teacher once called me a "rebellious, incorrigible cur." I continue to appreciate the fact that he, at least, helped me increase my vocabulary. *Cur*, I learned, is a scruffy stray dog. But I don't believe that was the spirit in which the commentary on my life was given.

"No one is able to bind them anymore." They are labeled brash, defiant, and out of control.

I feel that both teachers wanted me to know I had little or no value to them. They had decided that I didn't count for much. They banned me to the margins of the classroom to focus their time on students who had a brighter future than my inevitable, hopeless outcome.

Street kids who lean up against the walls of businesses along Seattle's streets have heard the voices of some who are like two of my former teachers. These kids are mirror images of the demon-possessed man in Mark's Gospel. They serve as constant reminders to the communities they drift through that no one is able to fix them. "No one is able to bind them anymore." They are labeled brash, defiant, and out of control.

Walter Brueggemann in *The Prophetic Imagination* claims that, "Hope is the refusal to accept the reading of reality which is the majority opinion; and one does this only at great political and existential risk." Hope, in the cemetery doesn't believe the voices of the crowd—the voices that believed that binding, controlling, or subduing the man was the only answer. Hope believes that the kids on our streets are not too far-gone. They're not already dead.

The Majority Doesn't Rule

➡ A while back, a young woman named WENDY read about Jesus washing the disciples' feet. Wendy, a street kid herself, was volunteering in New Horizons Ministries' self-care center where the kids can get a hot shower, do laundry, and get clean socks and clothes. "Jesus washed the disciples' feet!" she exclaimed. "You should do this 'cause I bet the street kids' feet are way dirtier than the disciples,' feet were" she told our chaplain,

Wendy intuitively knew what the Public Health Department can confirm. In Seattle, foot problems are a major issue in the lives of homeless people. A wet climate guarantees wet socks. Leather boots that don't breathe, wet sneakers that don't dry out, plus walking all day is a recipe for fungus, blisters, and other forms of what the kids simply call foot rot. Living in squats (abandoned buildings) that are littered with needles and broken glass perpetuate the problem. A person simply doesn't take off smelly shoes to sleep in an abandoned building or you might wake up with no shoes at all. All of this adds up to feet that are wet, blistered, and infected.

So New Horizons' chaplain took Wendy's advice. He created a foot-washing night, complete with soft music, dim lights, and comfy couches that served as a waiting room. The chaplain, with the help of a few volunteer outreach workers, began to invite kids two by two to listen to the story of Jesus washing the disciples' feet. Each kid sat in front of a little tub and the volunteers took off dirty socks, scrubbed pairs of feet in warm soapy water, peeled away calluses, and applied ointment to infected wounds. Each kid was given a dry, warm towel and a new pair of socks. The kids, who had been hesitant initially, walked away refreshed—and some even began to ask our chaplain and his volunteer crew, "Hey, if you can wash my feet, can I tell you about this thing that I've carried—it's way dirtier than my feet." The kids began to share parts of their lives more wounded than their blistered feet.

The other amazing affect of foot washing was the impact that the ritual had on the perspective of New Horizons' volunteers. As they knelt down to wash the feet of young people almost their same age, they began to see the youth from a new perspective. The power that is so unequally distributed in our culture between black and white, male and female, rich and poor, felt like it shifted. The youth were not just getting their feet washed; their dreams and plans were being recognized.

Later the volunteers sat in our staff meeting and claimed that they were beginning to see the kids as more than a social problem to be solved. They told stories of simply listening as they peeled away calluses. They heard the youths' dreams of college. As the volunteers put ointment on infected sores, they heard stories of the wounds that led the kids to the streets. "These kids," the volunteers said, "are more beautiful and courageous than we had ever realized."

For a few minutes the voice of the dominant culture was quieted, and the prophetic voice of these kids' dreams, courage and pain was recognized. *Hope is the refusal to accept the majority opinion.*

➡ New Horizons has a retired surgeon, **Bob**, who volunteers as an outreach worker. He lives in a beautiful home on Puget Sound that served as an oasis from the huge demands of a life given to surgery. Now it serves as an oasis for a bunch of street kids.

The smell of barbeque wafts through the air as the kids spill out of a van. The sound of Nelly, Usher, and Tupac bounce off the water from a stereo far more familiar with Frank Sinatra. And the kids forget their troubles for a while, throw a Frisbee, and laugh. In the middle of all this is, Bob, the retired doctor whose actions speak loud to the kids. He welcomes them as if they were grandchildren. He refuses to believe the majority opinion, and now children who usually sit on the curbs downtown have a chance to sit on his grass and enjoy sunshine and home. When these kids move away from the insanity of the streets, they begin to be seen as just kids wanting to be kids. *Hope is the refusal to believe the majority of opinion.*

➡ A contractor, another **BOB**, came to our office one day, his dream was simply to hire youth from New Horizons to renovate and sell houses. Many of the older kids who need gainful employment have a very difficult time finding and maintaining a job. His dream of hiring street youth might sound more like a nightmare to the majority of employers.

A few weeks later, after ironing out a lot of the details, one of our kids strolled in for an interview with a 20-ounce soft drink in his hand and his mouth stained with chips. He drifted into an office with the contractor. He looked back and said, "This job is mine."

Everything was wrong. The kid was not ready for a job and the builder had no idea what he was asking for. This was going to be one of those, I-told-you-so moments. But all outward appearances can be wrong; two years later the young man is still working for his builder friend. Bob has a son who refers to their "adopted" street kid as his uncle. Oh, there have been some challenges. But the point is the contractor refused to believe this kid couldn't do it. *Hope is the refusal to believe the majority opinion.*

A Better Way

The most amazing thing about Jesus in the cemetery story is that, in His deliverance, He never used the binding language of the crowd or the demon. Jesus refused to believe that simply subduing a man in a cemetery a safe distance from the community was the answer.

Jesus refused to believe the crowd—the majority opinion. Instead, He looked beyond the soul of a tormented man into a heart of one created by God. Each time we sit at the kids' feet, share a meal, give them a chance to share their dreams, the voice of the dominant culture is quieted just enough to see who these kids were created to be. We make radical choices that don't seem like economic sense. We are not saying the problems

How do we get to a point where hope refuses to submit to the language of oppression, the majority of opinion.

are serious, we are saying that Jesus has revealed a better way, a way that might not be so dependant on binding or subduing. The question is how do we get to a point where hope refuses to submit to the language of oppression, the majority of opinion, the voice that claims some kids are just too broken, too far-gone.

Created in His Image

➡ While traveling through India, I was able to visit the Sisters of Charity's home for the sick and dying in Bombay. This is the order of Catholic sisters established by the late Mother Teresa. As we walked through the compound, my colleagues and I would stop and shake the hand of an old man or play with a baby that lay in a crib. We entered one dormitory that housed young women who looked to be in latter adolescence.

The dorm mother said these women had been there since birth. They were crippled and had been abandoned in the hospital. As we began to make our way around the dorm, one severely deformed young woman caught my eye.

Her forehead was enlarged. She had no eyes, simply dark holes where her eyes should have been. She suffered from a cleft pallet. Her nose, mouth, teeth, and gums joined together in such a way that they were almost indistinguishable features. Her chin was almost as large as her forehead. She looked horrible to me. I tried to move on, but God clearly impressed me to stop with these words:

Don't move! Capture her face in your mind's eye. Almost immediately, she began to sing. "I have joy that the world didn't give me, and the world can't take it away. I have peace that the world didn't give me, and the world can't take it away." As I continued to look, I felt an immense distance from God. As I heard the joy in her voice, I began to realize the young woman's beauty was hidden from me. I was the one who was blind, unable to see this woman made in the image of God.

Her face only served as a reminder of all things broken in this world. I, like the crowd in Mark's story, had this evil instinct to keep her face a safe distance from me where I could act as if it did not exist. I had listened to the voice of the dominant culture and decided this young woman was ugly. The more I looked at her the more I realized this young woman was only blind to the evil opinions that suffocate hope and deny the beautiful image of God revealed in her. As I walked away, I wondered how I could be so arrogant as to think I could preach the gospel to people if I could not recognize the image of God in them.

What could I say to the people I wanted to push to the margins of my community or the margins of my memory? Unless I can look through all the brokenness and see the image of God, I have nothing. No vision, no hope. You see, the Sisters of Charity have hope because they refuse to believe the majority of opinion about this young woman and so many others.

At New Horizons Ministries I am amazed by the people who stand in defiance to the voices that declare kids living on the streets are not salvageable. Many of the staff have also seen the graffiti, maybe not physically since it has been painted over, but they've heard it in the voices of the dominant culture that question the kids' value. They have heard it, but they refuse to believe it. The staff has dug deep enough to see the created beauty in all the street kids. They reflect the attitude of Jesus when He looked—not around but beyond tormented souls and proclaimed that those who sit on the margins of our culture and on our city curbs are created in the image of God.

I don't know the name of the young woman I met in Bombay, but I will never forget her face, and I will never forget her song. A song that confronted me with my own blindness, my inability to see her created in the image of God. A song that confronted me with my own propensity to push away all that reminds me of my inability to fix things. A song that let me know I have a ways to go if I hope to see these kids the way God sees them—created in His image.

"In the beginning God created…"
—GENESIS 1:1

9

Created
in the Image
of God

I AM ALWAYS SURPRISED THAT OUR PHILOSOPHY FOR LOVING the world doesn't more often start here. I think many of us as Christians are far more familiar with John 3:16 as an evangelical text, but I have come to believe that the good news of God reaching out to His creation starts with *"In the beginning..."* This Genesis story is more than proof that God created all things. It speaks to how our identity should be shaped and helps us to understand our God-given purpose in the world.

Most Christians believe that they know the creation story, but often when I ask Christian college students to tell me how the creation story begins, someone usually starts out by saying, "God tells Eve not to eat of the tree of knowledge." The story doesn't start with a *don't*; it actually starts with affirmations of our identity and invites us to participate in God's purpose for the world. My friend Bob Eckblad does a great job with the Creation story in his book, *Reading the Bible with the Damned*.

The Creation story begins with a loving Father giving birth to His creation and providing everything that the new creation needs to thrive. His command to not eat from the tree of knowledge is given with the motivation of a loving parent. It's not the story of God who wants to maintain control; it's the story of God who wants to protect the innocence of His creation.

Whether you are a Bible college student, an inmate at the county jail, or a young person living on the street, human inclination is to get stuck on what we're being told not to do, not on all the things we can do. For some reason we gravitate to the one *don't* in the story of Adam and Eve and manage to overlook the profound purpose of creation.

I am learning that when I want to tell kids on the street about the grand story of God, it helps to start with, "In the beginning..." I don't start with the creation story in order to prove the existence of God. Kids need the truth story because it speaks to a loving, creative God. However, far too often the kids on the street perceive God and God's power exemplified in unjust court systems, unethical police officers, dishonorable social workers, and manipulative Christians. They view God as having power and manipulating the world to please Himself. They do not see God acting out of love to create humans into a reflection of Himself so that we may reflect God's generosity and desire for community. We are made in God's image to reflect the beauty and power of God and to be creative as He is creative. We are given power that enables us to lead and steward God's resources, and we are told to eat abundantly from the garden because we serve an abundant God. The life we live in the world should exemplify our understanding that we have been created with purpose. But how do we help young people understand what being created in the image of God entails?

Rethinking Authority

All of us were created in God's image. Regardless of what mess we find ourselves in, or our painful history, we were made in God's image. We were created to lead, have dominion, and to live a life of abundance in Him. This word *dominion* doesn't mean "to dominate," but rather to be a steward over resources in the way God manages the world. It is in this image: bearing, stewarding, and eating abundantly that the story of God and the story of humankind should begin. In the beginning God created us. God wanted to be with us and for us to share in all that God is. If understanding this is hard for those of us in the dominant culture, imagine how hard it is for kids on the street.

Their family history is one of abuse and violence. They have been tossed into state systems that have little capacity to care for them. After 12 to 13 failed foster-care placements, and a few group homes, they run to the street. Actually, they run away from all the dysfunction and end up on the street. All the authority figures that they come into contact with seem harsh and demanding. How do they, as homeless youth in pain and trying to survive, think about who they were created to be? And how do they rethink images of authority and power that have too often been manipulative and punitive? Those of us who work with kids on the street must wrestle with the idea that the kids must find a place where they can discover that they bear the image of God. I believe as young people discover their talents, strengths, and assets through the programs at New Horizons that this is the place to help them rethink the creation story and help them discover how they fit into the plans of God.

In my experience working at New Horizons, I have come to believe that young people don't move off the streets in order to relinquish a bad habit. Presenting kids with messages like: "Don't use drugs" or "You shouldn't be homeless because it's wrong to commit crimes to survive" doesn't have the positive effect of moving kids forward. I've seen kids move beyond the street when they begin to discover who they were created to be. Kids are motivated to make change when they discover their gifts, strengths, and talents; and they move towards community when they realize they have something to give—not just something to get rid of, like addictions. Young people need to experience firsthand that the streets are a hindrance to their creative abilities and desires.

More than Softball

I began by doing recreation activities that later evolved into the New Horizons Life Discovery program, started at a local sporting goods store. I had been given the task of putting seven Stanford University students to work at New Horizons for a summer internship. What do you do with college students who will only be around for the summer? I decided that we could start playing softball once a week with the kids. Seven students would at least give me a critical mass to get a game going. I envisioned piling kids into volunteers' cars to transport them to the field, and coordinating with a volunteer food group to provide the BBQ dinner. The only problem was equipment.

My budget was a total of $15. I walked to the local sporting goods store and bought a wooden softball bat and 12 softballs. Let the season begin! Volunteers brought what gloves they had, and we shared as best we could. It was a great summer and softball turned into an annual summer event that kids looked forward to each year. Not only did the event provide kids fun away from the street, but it gave young people—who sold their bodies in order to survive—a few minutes each week just to be kids on the baseball diamond. Kids picked and managed their own teams, created a batting order, and designated positions. Kids learned to succeed and fail in a safe, fun environment. I remember one kid in particular: Drew.

➡️ At age 17, **DREW** was 6-feet-2-inches tall, and he weighed 210 pounds. His family suffered the painful effects of alcoholism, and he had spent most of his adolescent life in group homes. His size and anger issues soon made it impossible for the staff of these homes to manage him and so, in the words of the State, he was *emancipated as an adult.* Set free by the system to manage his own affairs, he quickly fell to the streets. Drew's lifelong dream was to sell commercial real estate.

On one occasion, New Horizons staff took the kids, including Drew, snowshoeing for the afternoon. At their arrival back in the city, we asked the kids what they had enjoyed about the trip. Without a second thought, Drew blurted out, "Driving through the industrial park in south Seattle." We had been in the Cascade Mountains all day but that scenery paled in comparison to seeing all those buildings beaming with potential.

Drew hadn't had much opportunity to play sports growing up, so playing softball was a new experience and often very frustrating for him. Many times he wouldn't get through an entire time at bat without exploding with rage, "My dad never showed me how to do this!" He would then proceed to scream, charge the mound, and look like he was plotting to take out the pitcher. The kids were great at talking him down, telling him not to worry about it, and stating that everyone has bad days! Yes, street kids de-escalated violent behavior. They would rally around Drew, letting him know he was OK. They told him that softball sucks anyway, and who cares if you're not any good at it?

> He wouldn't get through an entire time at bat without exploding with rage, "My dad never showed me how to do this!"

One night we had a real game against a local Rotary Club. It gave the kids a chance to interact with business people in a neutral environment. Most kids sit in front of businesses, begging for spare change, until they are chased away by the owner or the police. Business people and street kids do not usually have a friendly relationship. But on this night we were playing the Rotary and eating really good BBQ. To be honest, it wasn't a very competitive game. New Horizons' kids were losing 12 or 13 to nothing. The 55-year-old Rotarians were calling the dogs off, and the kids had resigned themselves to the fact that we were going to lose again. But the food was better than it had been all summer, so everything was bearable. It was probably the sixth inning of a seven-inning softball game when something magical happened. The street kids had a little rally going on. After a quick two outs, we had runners on base. Not a runner but runners—plural! Can you guess who was up next? Yes, Drew.

The other kids tried to remain positive. They *were* positive; positive Drew would never hit the ball. I was coaching third base, and I remember moving a little closer to the pitcher, fearing Drew would attack the mound as well as the nice woman pitcher. Kids in the dugout began, for safety's sake, to gather up the extra bats and balls. This could be a disaster. Drew swung a couple of times and the oblivious Rotarians cheered him on. Little did they know they were pouring kerosene in the smoldering fire of Drew's emotional pain. The New Horizons first base coach started to walk towards the plate, hoping to catch Drew before he took out the woman who was now calling him *honey* and telling him that she knew he could do it. She obviously didn't know what all of us knew!

If I hadn't experience firsthand what happened next, I never would have believed it. It was sincerely a faith-building moment—for us like water made into wine—the parting of the Red Sea. Drew hit the ball! Drew hit the ball with the most unorthodox swing I had ever witnessed. The ball flew hard to left field. Thankfully, New Horizons could not rent a good field and the free park baseball diamond had a severe downhill slope moving to a patch of trees. The Rotarian playing left field didn't have a chance.

Drew took off; he rounded first, and tumbled toward second. Then...he stopped! I was coaching third base and screamed, "Run, Drew, run!" It was at that point that I realized he had never seen the world from second base before. This was a new perspective on baseball, and life for that matter. He wanted to stop and enjoy the view; savor the moment. But, thankfully, Drew quickly realized this was no time to stop. He ran past me and on through third. The kids were climbing the dugout fence. The Rotarian's arm was no better than his legs. Drew crossed home plate as the ball dribbled across the mound. It was a day of rejoicing! I am talking, unbridled joy, the old-time Christian camp meeting type of joy. Kids hugging staff, staff hugging kids, barbecue thrown everywhere. Joy! Drew had hit a home run, after weeks of frustration and moments of rage. Drew had walked up to the plate and did it. It felt great!

Did this event tell Drew who he was created to be? Well, probably not. But for a moment everything stopped. All the accusations, all the fear of failure, all the memories of an isolated childhood left alone to figure things out on his own. For a second it stopped. Drew was able to look back and make sense of all the nights at softball. He was able to see that he could do it. He felt what it was like to be part of a community, to do something that contributed to a whole family of folks.

We lost the game. I think the final score was 13–3. But Drew was a hero.

When he applies for a job or enrolls in school, he will have a point of reference other than a childhood filled with empty promises, disappointment, and alcoholism. Drew has another snapshot. A snapshot that is different than the family pictures he has in his memory. Drew was able to risk a lot in a safe, supportive environment where other kids coached and encouraged him to keep trying. Drew now has a memory of a day when he did something great, a memory that says he's not a failure. He is made in the image of God, leading, and enjoying plenty of success, the fruit of his labor. What started as a summer of softball has evolved into an entire Life Discovery Program activity that helps kids discern their gifts and talents.

Today, if you were to walk into New Horizons, you might not walk into a softball game, but you might see kids cooking, taking computer classes, participating in a writing group, or a women's self-defense class. You might hear kids talking about a recent field trip to talk with a local business owner, or their visit to an art gallery. You would see kids paired up with John, the facilities manager; Rudy, the information technology coordinator; and you would witness kids answering phones with Sara, New Horizons' agency administrator.

You might hear the voice of New Horizons' Life Discovery coordinator, Octaiviea, as she invites a young person to an activity saying, "How do you know? Maybe you would be really good at it. Maybe you wouldn't be good at it, but it's worth the risk."

"Let us, then, go to him outside the camp, bearing the disgrace he bore."
—HEBREWS 13:12–13

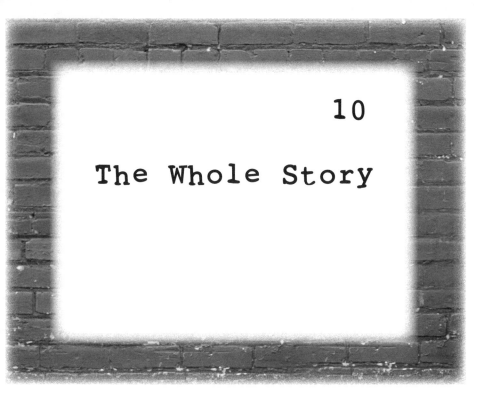

10

The Whole Story

I RECENTLY VISITED GUATEMALA CITY, WHERE 4 MILLION people live. Joel, one of my doctoral students, invited me. He and I met at a training put on by a group called the Center for Transforming Mission (CTM). CTM is an organization that equips young leaders to serve youth and families in tough places around the world. Joel became the Latin American Director. When Joel was going through Bakke Graduate School, I was a professor for an independent study class. The curriculum meant he attended New Horizons Ministries' volunteer training—to observe lay training and to do pastoral care with high-risk young people. Joel hoped to gain methods to enhance the ministries of Guatemalan leaders working with gang-involved youth and street youth. Joel serves as Director of the Strategy of Transformation (the name in Latin America for the work of CTM because of its partnership with Christian Reformed World Missions).

Strategy of Transformation is "the Barnabas"—encouragers to the Guatemalan grassroots leaders who are serving their own people in really hard places, like gang-involved youth, street youth, and those in prisons in Guatemala City and its surrounding area. My visit to Guatemala was to be the final phase of his independent study. While there, I would observe his work in his context and discuss how New Horizons' training strategies fit within it. We would delve into how training, practice, and theological reflection could further equip the chaplains and youth workers Joel's work supports, and enhance his volunteer training program.

My son Clayton gave me a fun-filled caution as he dropped me off for my flight to Guatemala: "Don't go down any dark alleys and make sure you practice *safe* theology." He knows inner-city challenges, not typical tourist attractions, draw me. Clayton loves to make fun in that way because he, too, has learned from living in our own neighborhood that places we feel are unattractive, unsafe, and unfamiliar can actually be places of immense beauty, comfort, and community. *Unsafe* cities provide an undeniable sense of God's power. Amidst people's pain and suffering we find the beauty of God's grace. In fact, cities provide places for incredible learning because these are places where brokenness cannot be masked by superficial beauty and a false sense of order.

Once in Guatemala City, I had the incredible privilege of seeing beautiful, powerful places and people. I spent time on the streets with street kids, and met an incredible man named Italo.

➡ He spends his nights driving city alleys, seeking children who make themselves scarce during the day. These children survive by inhaling cheap glue in order to suppress their appetite—and their pain. ITALO welcomed each kid with an incredible greeting, "Hello, beautiful creations of God." He hugs, plays, and dances on the streets with them.

Their eyes once dulled by deadly inhalants come alive when he reaches out to them.

⇨ I also met TITA, a woman who runs a school for children in a community full of tin shacks built on the steep hills of a ravine. She serves the La Limonada community of about 55,000 people—35,000 of them children. This city within the city is thought by many to be a place of shame due to the immense poverty its conditions reveal. There's no clean drinking water, there are major sanitation problems, makeshift electricity, and the neighborhood is considered very dangerous. Two hundred fifty kids now attend Tita's two schools. When she walks the streets, women, men, and children all run to greet her with a hug and a smile. As she walks, she stops to kiss each child. She has no formal education; she tells me she was educated on her knees. When I asked her about the requirements for volunteers who would serve with her, she said with a laugh, "Give me crazy people who love Jesus." She is the Mother Teresa of Guatemala City and everyone in the neighborhood responds to her loving embrace.

As a result of a consultation on street gang outreach in 2005, the group Joel directs was asked to help spearhead a gang chaplaincy initiative into the maximum security gang units of Guatemala's prison system. While I was there, we visited a young man who had just become a Christian, and who at the risk of losing his life was walking away from gang affiliation. He was being transferred from a prison that housed his fellow gang members to a prison specifically designed for men leaving the gangs and those inmates who had never had any gang affiliation.

In the prison system, gang members are at the bottom rung. Gang members are usually housed in separate prisons on isolated units with other members of their same gangs because of the way they are demonized (or marginalized) by society at large and even within the walls of the prison system. Even if you've walked away from gang activity, everyone is skeptical of you. Inmates of the prison system who have never been involved with gangs consider it an honor to kill an inmate who's been a gang member. It doesn't matter if you're a current gang member or a former gang member; it's sometimes considered a badge of honor to assassinate an inmate who's been affiliated at one time or another with a gang. The young man had changed prisons, left the gang, and converted to Christianity—he was still a long way from being safe.

➡️ I went to the prison with **JOEL**, one of the chaplains in the chaplaincy initiative that he serves, and a young ex-gang member, turned Christian, whom this chaplain was discipling. Every time former gang members walk back into the prison system, they place their own lives at risk since they are no longer affiliated with their gangs and, therefore, have no community to protect them. This adds to the danger of their potential death. Joel and the group he directs try to support the Guatemalan chaplains in their own ministries with resources, some training, and a place in the missional community that is his network.

I was dependent on Joel and the Guatemalan men that day. Their English was much better than my Spanish and we began to discuss where we were heading. Alvin told me, "This is the end of the line. These guys who have left the gangs or have been thrown out would not last a day on the streets. Life in the prison is much safer than freedom on the streets." The man that we were going to see could not trust a single person in his world. He had risen to power and in doing so had threatened some other members in the gang structure. The details of his departure from the gang were foggy. The man we were to visit had attempted to create better living conditions for the men in his unit, interacted and worked closely with prison administration, and now was out of the gang unit and all alone. Somewhere along the line, his gang brothers that he was advocating for felt like his allegiance to the institution was a form of betrayal and threatened his life.

➡ **ALVIN** began to tell me his own story. He was from a very poor neighborhood and had only been a chaplain about a year. At this point, his English speaking fell short and Joel began to interpret Alvin's story. He grew up in the garbage dumps of Guatemala City. An infamous Central American gang had recruited him at such an early age; he really couldn't remember how old he had been when he had joined. He grew up in an area with no plumbing, hospital, or schools—sustained on dangerous homemade electricity. His gang was the closest thing his neighborhood had to a police department. The gang protected his family and became his brothers. He told me that by age 15 he was tired of the wars, the politics, and searching for something else. He told me, "I met a preacher who told me all the evil could be washed away by Jesus. I gave my heart to Jesus and I promised to follow His ways."

Sören Kierkegaard says admirers always keep their distance but followers move close enough to be transformed by the experience.

One of my dear friends and mentors, Tony, tells me Christians are more than admirers; they are Jesus followers. He always quotes Sören Kierkegaard. He claims there is a big difference between Jesus *followers* and *admirers*. He says admirers always keep their distance but followers move close enough to be transformed by the experience. Alvin would make Kierkegaard and Tony proud. He's a true follower. He went on to tell me that, sometimes, if you are truly converted, your gang won't kill you but will let you live a religious life separate from the gang. He explained that you had to present your case to the leader and confess your faith. The gang leader would then decide as to whether your faith was authentic or only a mere ploy to get you out of some element of gang trouble.

As I continued to listen, I was amazed at how Alvin told his story of life and death in such a simple and matter-of-fact fashion. To my mind, it was like, *Oh, by the way, I left the gang and they decided not to kill me.* I asked, "Alvin, how did you decide to make this public confession? Why didn't you decide to just be a nicer gang member? You know, keep your faith personal? Jesus is a personal Savior isn't He? Why weren't you more cautious; this is your life you're talking about? Alvin looked at me and in the same matter-of-fact tone said, "I read the story in the Bible about Paul being in prison. He wasn't afraid. He said to live is Christ, to die is gain. I believe the Bible." Alvin's voice became filled with joy. "I read it and I knew I would win either way. If I live, I'll tell everyone that Jesus washed my sins away. If I die, I am with Him. See, Ron, I win. You win either way."

I was embarrassed as I questioned whether or not I really believed that verse, I know I didn't believe it at least the way Alvin believed. He knew Philippians 1:21, "For to me, living is Christ and dying is gain." Paul pens these lines while he is in prison in Rome. Some scholars argue Philippians is Paul's last correspondence before he dies. Alvin believed this like Paul believed it. He was filled with conviction.

As we continued our drive toward the prison, we passed open fields. Beautiful greens that turned almost blue in the Guatemalan sunlight. The beauty of the countryside made me forget where we were heading. How could the prison be that bad of a place when the scenery was so gorgeous? We finally arrived at the huge structure that was our destination and parked in a dusty pothole-filled lot. I stood in front of a stone structure that looked like it was built in the 1800s, thinking, *this is really a prison*. It looked nothing like the prisons back home.

A line was forming outside a ten-foot-high iron gate. All of us walked toward the line: Joel, a missionary from Michigan; a former gang member and a man who hoped to become a chaplain; and me. I sure didn't feel very theologically astute after my car ride with Alvin. He had already taught me a lot. The line was filled with old men and women, small children, and well-dressed younger women. Some of them fathers, some of them mothers, some of them sons, daughters, wives, or girlfriends—all were waiting to visit someone in prison. Men don't often visit other men in prison, at least not in groups of four. Immediately, we were pulled out of line. We definitely stood out.

Joel explained to the guard that while we didn't have a chaplaincy pass for this specific prison, we wanted to visit a young man that he knew from another institution. Joel told the guard that we had an American who wanted to visit the prison. That was me. We were rushed off to the warden's office. We passed the front of the line and I was wondering if this was a good thing. On our way through the gate, David, the other chaplain, walked over and had a short conversation with an inmate. When he caught up with us, Joel asked him how he knew this guy. David told us that this guy was a warden just three or four weeks ago. Now he was doing time like any other inmate. David commented that he had probably forgotten to pay somebody off. This place seemed crazy and I didn't know the rules.

Inside Others' Contexts

We got into the warden's office and a long conversation in Spanish ended with smiles and handshakes. Joel said that the warden claimed that he was happy to have religious services for the men, and was incredibly glad that a doctor from the United States was investing in the young men of Guatemala, because he, like me, was hoping they would be rehabilitated. He told one his guards that we should be given access to any inmate with whom we wanted to talk. We thanked him for taking time to meet with us and granting us such access. I guess I was earning my keep. My status as an American and my credentials meant the prison warden wanted to impress me. This was embarrassing, but I knew that I was a man of privilege and I might as well use it for something good. We left the warden's office and I started to think to myself, *This isn't so bad.*

Wardens like to impress visitors, especially European-American ones from the US. He might have been genuine in his concern for the inmates' rehabilitation, and the prison seemed safe enough. Lots of guards, clean-looking warden's building, and well-manicured grass. About this time, we reach another gate. We left our IDs with another guard who sat in a shack. I started to feel uncomfortable with the thought of leaving my passport while at the same time going into a prison. The gate we were about to enter resembled the original iron gate that we first entered through. This one, however, was twice as big and wrapped with barbed wire. I reluctantly relinquished my passport and walked through. I heard the creek of the gate and, as it closed, I realized all the uniformed men were standing outside the walled area we were passing through. I was struck suddenly with cold, sobering thoughts, *All the corrections officers on the perimeter of a prison.*

I stood with Joel, Alvin, David, and a lot of men looking for their mothers, sons, daughters, or wives. As we walked through the prison yard, I looked to find the guards. Thoughts of my passport being sold before I could get back to the gate distracted me.

➡️ SOME OF THE MALE PRISONERS played soccer. Some cut large coconuts with even larger homemade machetes. Others sold soda pop and thirst quenchers. Now this is where I have to admit that stereotypes and profiling get in the way of reality. I looked at machetes and food and drink available with little security and I immediately landed on Hollywood images. I began to wonder if this was like the movies. What I didn't know until later: all this freedom was earned by men, many of whom were a few steps way from freedom and moving back into the community. This wasn't atypical, and chaos didn't rule. But all the images

Roberto was a high-ranking gang official. In the previous prison, Roberto had become frustrated with the lack of activity provided.

were strange to me and I had no point of reference to interpret or understand. I was not in a context I understood. As we approached a large building that I assumed was the housing unit, a man came running toward David and Alvin. He hugged them both. I thought, *This must be who we came to see.* I was then introduced to Roberto. I tried hard to pay attention to the introduction. I pushed away the thoughts of my passport being sold and attempted to focus.

➡️ I knew a little of **ROBERTO'S** story. The chaplains briefed me regarding the details of Roberto's predicament. Chaplains had met him in another prison. Roberto was a high-ranking gang official. In the previous prison, Roberto had become frustrated with the lack of activity provided for the inmates and began to create a document that would address the spiritual, physical, and education needs of his brothers in the prison. Back home, before I had come to Guatemala, Joel had given me a copy of the document. It was incredibly thorough and well written. One could easily see Roberto's organizational skills. The only problem with his plan was that the prison administration loved it. They loved it so much that they began to delegate to Roberto other administrative tasks. Soon his gang affiliates became suspicious of his allegiance to the "police" and ordered him killed, thinking he was turning against them. He was crushed by their accusations and then had to make the most difficult choice of his life—ask for a transfer or die.

Roberto spoke only Spanish and Joel was very kind to keep me somewhat up to speed as we began to have a conversation together. We pushed a few dogs out of some plastic lawn chairs and sat down while Roberto brought each of us a Gatorade. (Remember, our wallets and ID were hopefully back in the guard shack.) Roberto told us of his transfer and of the incredible loneliness and depression that came with his being moved out of the gang unit and being labeled a traitor. In the middle of his loneliness, he had begun to read the Bible and had asked God to give him a purpose to live. Roberto said that he thought of suicide many times. But as he prayed to God, he also thought about the poor in Guatemala and the lack of resources to available to help them. He was especially concerned about those with major medical problems.

An amazing story followed. The prison he was currently in was a city unto itself. As I sat there, sipping an ice-cold Gatorade, he began to tell me that when he first arrived he realized that there were many cottage industries established by the inmates in the main yard. There were soda pop and beverage stands, live chickens for sale, and a variety of food items for sale that supplemented the prison-issued rice and beans. Roberto noticed that they had everything except a tortilla stove. He began talking with the other Christian inmates and through the missional network, obtained the stove. They began to sell tortillas to the other inmates. They produced volumes of tortillas that generated several hundred dollars of profit. They started to think about where they could donate the money.

Cell phones are everywhere in the Guatemalan prison system. I guess it's a lot better than the US system, where inmates call collect or must create a bank of minutes to be used with preapproved visitors. I am sure lots of phone companies benefit. Roberto and his fellow inmates started making calls, searching for churches that knew of children who were sick with cancer. After lots of phone calls, they finally identified two needy families who had children with terminal illnesses. They made arrangements to invite the families to the prison and then presented all the money they had raised from the tortilla stand to them. They told the families that, even though they were in prison, they realized they were blessed, and if they were truly Christians they must share this blessing with others.

The strategy to purchase an oven, sell tortillas, and find recipients for the profits involved complex and elaborate planning. As Roberto told the story, he was so proud of the great project that they had created. He looked at me and said in Spanish, "Even though we are in prison, as Christians we must care for those that have less than we do." I sat there listening to the story interpreted into English. I continued to listen as Roberto shared about his plans to do even more. I thought back to the human services plan that Roberto had authored. He was truly a gifted organizer and administrator. When there was a break in the conversation, I took the opportunity to quickly look through the Spanish Bible sitting on the table next to us. I was looking for the story of Joseph in Genesis 18. I found it, but in this Bible, it was the story of Jose. After finding the chapter I asked Roberto, "Have you ever read this story?" He shook his head and said, "No." Through Joel I began to recount the story.

Divine Connections

"Roberto, I saw the proposal you created to give your fellow inmates more access to recreational, religious, and social services. I have listened to you share about your tortilla business that you created to raise money to help families with very sick children. The business you developed not only helped children, but also gave the inmates in this prison a sense of purpose. Joseph in Genesis 18 was also a gifted organizer and administrator. He not only saved his family, but the entire nation of Egypt through his administrative gifts. Roberto, you're like Joseph."

All of a sudden, Alvin became incredibly excited and began to share something with Roberto. Since they were speaking in Spanish, I was in the dark. Alvin kept grabbing the Bible and telling Roberto something. Roberto kept laughing and clapping. Joel began to tell me what was happening. Alvin knew the story of Joseph as well. As I had begun to compare Roberto's gifts to those of Joseph, Alvin became filled with the Spirit and started to preach the following message:

> Roberto, you, like Joseph, have a gift that made your brothers jealous. Joseph's brothers threw him in a hole; your brothers threatened to kill you. Joseph was sold by his brothers into slavery; you were banished from the former gang prison, sent to another prison meant for those who have nowhere else to go. But God gave Joseph *favor*. What his brothers meant for evil, God intended for good. This is your story, Roberto. God has brought you here! Formerly you were in a prison cell with 125 fellow gang members and now you're in a prison where you have influence over 500! God has taken evil and made it good for you!" Roberto found himself in the story of Joseph that day. He was ready to

usher us out early just so he could sit alone and read the story of Joseph for himself.

The story of God's faithfulness to both Joseph and Roberto is a divine connection we all had the privilege to witness. We experienced that "thin place" in the supernatural, where God's light is revealed in a very dark place mysteriously. During that afternoon visit, we all had participated in the telling of the story of Joseph *and* the story of Roberto. God used me to bring the story to the table, but Joel had interpreted, and a former gang member had illuminated and contextualized the story in a profound way. Two gang members, a missionary, and I unwrapping a piece of Scripture together in a Guatemalan prison—amazing!

What are the parts of the Bible to which we are blind, based on our limited experiences of God?

As I rode away from the prison, I thought of all of us who had sat at the table. I thought to myself, *it truly takes a whole community to tell the whole story of God.* Joel, I, Alvin, David, and Roberto had all contributed in the mysterious God-moment. The profound story of God beautifully interwoven and connected with a story of a man, banished from his gang of brothers only to find himself in the story of Joseph. Thrown into a prison of refugees only to organize, administer his gifts, and bring hope through his abilities. The whole story of God can only be experienced in that way when we're together as a whole community.

Today, I continue to wonder how often we as Christians hear only part of the story. What are the parts of the Bible to which we are blind, based on our limited experiences of God? I also know that most of our Christian communities could benefit from hearing voices like Alvin's and Roberto's. These men are not usually invited to the community to share their theological perspectives or experiences. Who have we ignored in God's community, and how has the story of God been limited because their voices have not been heard? My time at the prison would have been much different without Alvin. I continue to challenge myself with this and other questions, in an effort to experience God's complete and whole community: *Who are those people in our church that need to be invited to speak? Who are those who are not currently being invited to share their stories of God?*

In him the whole building is joined together
and rises to become a holy temple in the Lord.
And in him you too are being built together
to become a dwelling in which
God lives by his Spirit.
—EPHESIANS 2:21–22

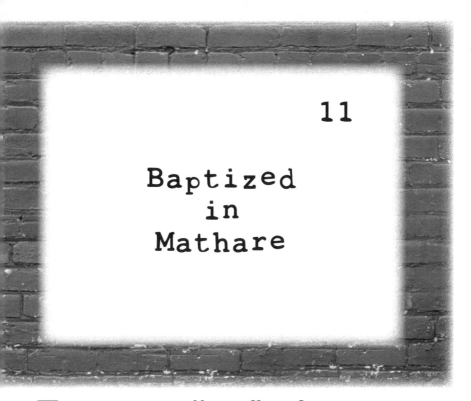

11

Baptized
in
Mathare

I T WAS MY LAST DAY IN NAIROBI, KENYA. I HAD BEEN THERE
teaching a class through the Center for Transforming
Mission (CTM). This amazing training organization
equips ministry practitioners and urban youth workers
to serve youth and families in really hard places. The
diversity of the students attending and the locations of
these conferences make the classes special and unique.
Classes have been held in prisons and diverse multicultural
urban neighborhoods across the world. These theological
meetings bring urban ministry practitioners, pastors, and
graduate-level students together to discuss what good news
is good news in hard places. As a former staff member
of New Horizons Ministries, I partner with CTM to help
provide these theological conferences. Bakke Graduate
School offers graduate-level accreditation for students who
request it.

One of the incredible students of our intensive in Nairobi
is a young man named Moses. We had become friends

during my visit, and as my trip was coming to an end he wanted to give me a tour of his community, Mathare.

Mathare can appear to be a tragic place. It's one of three informal settlements or slum communities that sit on the outskirts of Nairobi. I have been told that sixty percent of Nairobi's residents live in these kinds of informal settlements. All of Mathare's 500,000 or more residents experience severe poverty and very primitive living conditions. These nearby settlements supply the endless sources of cheap labor required to sustain Nairobi's economy. The hardworking people of Mathare and the other internal settlements walk miles and miles to low-paying jobs, to keep the city of Nairobi moving.

The settlement of Mathare sits in a valley and is divided by a river running north to south. Like the word implies, slums worldwide are located in the most undesirable places. The community was originally set up in this location because the settlement lays in a ravine that floods during the rainy season. On the day I visited, the river that cuts through the community was running fast with raw sewage and garbage. Several men sat on the riverbank making *chang'aa*, an illegal liquor that is supplied to all of Nairobi. The men work 24 hours a day, seven days a week, to keep up with the demand. No one knows exactly how much illegal booze they produce, but it moves out in plastic two-gallon jugs as quickly as it can be bottled. The river is also the center of activity for women and children. The kids play and the women wash upstream as the human waste of 500,000 people floats by. There are few public bathrooms in Mathare, and once I walked into one I realized why the children urinate on the riverbank.

Inspiration

➡ Moses grew up in Mathare and now runs a ministry called Inspiration. He and his staff don't earn a salary or run their programs from funds from foundations or churches. They truly trust God for their day-to-day resources. Moses and his staff do street outreach, run a drop-in center for children in the settlement, and have a computer lab set up in the bottom floor of a neighboring apartment building. It could accurately be described as a closet with four computers. It's clear that Moses and his staff are doing a lot with very little.

The drop-in center is a concrete room, maybe 8-by-12-feet. Moses walked over to the drum set that sits in the corner and began to play. Instantly, kids from all over the neighborhood came to the drop-in center. They danced and laughed, and for a second I forgot it was an 8-by-12 concrete room. I met MICHAEL, one of Moses' co-workers. He was once a street kid in Mathare, but he now runs a shoeshine business to raise money for the kids served by Inspiration and to support himself.

As I walked the streets of Mathare with my CTM colleagues, it was obvious that Moses and Michael were known, loved, and trusted pastors of their community. The children gathered close to Moses and Michael; they felt safe in the shadow of these two men. Walking and talking, Michael told me about having lived on the streets as a kid. He said once a group of Christians bought him a shoeshine kit. It was that act of kindness that helped him survive. Now he uses that same kit to serve other street boys. Michael's business office is on the side of a dusty road on the edge of this garbage-filled community. As men walk out of the community to work in the city, Michael shines their shoes, preparing them to work downtown, and earning income for Inspiration.

As we continued through Mathare, we stopped at the shell of a burnedout shack. Moses and Michael told me that during the post-election violence a man was burned alive. The election was filled with corruption and tribal implications. The burned-out shack is only one example of the terror that filled the informal settlements. Many people say the chaos was forced on the settlements by the rich, because these settlements and the residents are seen as expendable. Whatever the reason, the fighting, the violence, the bloodshed, and death have disproportionately fallen on the backs of the poor.

We crossed a bridge that looked about half-complete. It hung above the river of sewage, and I was very thankful for it. As we looked over the poor community, the funky, sewage-filled river slowly moved below us. Moses asked, "Are you willing to be baptized in that river?"

A group of children had started walking with us and were chanting *"Monzooka, monzooka, monzooka."* I am a *monzooka*, a "white man." It was their playful warning to anyone that might be unaware that this man was in their neighborhood.

We stopped at the edge of the community and stood on the highest point of the settlement. From here we could see the entire Mathare community. Moses said that many street boys had died in this place. The papers reported that a street gang of 15 dangerous young men were killed by police in a fierce gun battle, but the people who lived here knew a different story. The incident involved 50 street boys who were unarmed and unaffiliated with any community—not gang-affiliated, just kids with no family, hanging out on the streets. It's said the boys were surrounded in this place and shot down. I thought, *No animal in the wild would be allowed such a fate.*

How Are You?

As we continued our tour, the children got more courageous and moved in closer to me. They practiced the one English phrase they knew, "How are you?" I answered that I was fine, but that didn't satisfy them. They continued asking, "How are you? How are you? How are you?" I was walking through Mathare wearing black boots, blue jeans, and a brown shirt. I looked like I was part of the cast of *Lost*, the hip sci-fi version of *Gilligan's Island*. I was so very North American US. I tried to be discreet but the kids knew the truth. I looked like a tourist in the middle of Africa. I think the children knew that being noticed and being cute was a chance to convince me that their neighborhood was worth caring about.

Michael and Moses told me story after story as the children continued to chirp, "How are you? How are you?" They were an army of little birds; ducklings that followed, and laughed, and continued to repeat the phrase over and over again. New little ones joined in, laughing at and following the *monzooka* and his tour guides.

I felt a tinge of guilt as I realized that a part of me was already gone. I was ready to go home.

The tour was coming to an end and I began to think just a quick decent down the hill, through the ravine, past the African moonshiners, up a trail filled with garbage, and then I would get on a plane and fly to Amsterdam. I felt a tinge of guilt as I realized that a part of me was already gone. I was ready to go home; I was ready to be done with all this.

When I snapped back to the present, I realized our bridge, my bridge, was gone! It hadn't been much, but it was a safe passage across the river that was flowing with disease. We had traveled about 400 yards upstream and this bridge was two piles of garbage and a rock blackened from the *chang'aa* brew. I begged Moses for an alternative. I am a 200-pound, 46-year-old, one-eyed man. I fell off the balance beam in first grade. The beam was two inches wide and three inches above a gym mat, and now you want me to jump across a river of bacteria. *No, this ain't gonna work.*

My two tour guides assured me that I would make it. My first leap was successful. I managed to land on a muddy pile of garbage in the middle of the water. I got ready to take my second jump, but I took too long and my left foot began to sink into the quicksand-type mud—I leapt, realized my jump was going to fall short, and my right boot began to fill with water and sewage. I released my left foot from the mud and fell forward, feeling a wave of refuse pour over my back. The back of my body was soaked. The "How are you?" chants of the children stopped immediately. For a moment everything was silent! Then my American colleague, Kris Rocke, executive director of CTM, started to laugh hysterically. Then the moonshiners started to laugh, then my tour guides, and then the children. Everyone was sharing in the guilty laughter. I had been baptized in the River of Mathare.

As we walked up the other side of the ravine, I thought about how much joy it brought the moonshiners to see me get so wet and stinky so fast. I was covered with the smell of what was wounded about this community. I could not hide the fact that I had been in Mathare. Moses and Michael said they were so sorry. As we walked up the hill I told them it wasn't their fault. Gideon, a Kenyan brother that accompanied us, told me that when a Kenyan says he's sorry, he's not taking blame, he's speaking with empathy. I was faced with the reality that my response had come from my hidden belief that their apology meant that they somehow had the power to take responsibility for my immersion into the filth of the river.

I realized at that moment that my motivation for saying sorry so much of the time is birthed out of my perceived power to somehow control the situations I'm in. My response comes from the power, guilt, and perceived responsibility that I carry with me as an AngloAmerican male, steeped with privilege. My African brothers weren't caught up in any of that. They knew they had no control over the event, and said they were sorry truly because they felt empathy.

I was struck again by the reality that my "Anglo-American male" culture means I bring my social location of power with me wherever I go. My status as such affects all of my responses. I must be intentional and aware of what that construct brings to my interactions around the world. How often do I unconsciously impose my power and social construct on the culture of others? I realized that the road of cultural competency involves a lifetime journey of learning.

My Kenyan colleague, PHILLIP, said, "Welcome to Africa!" and pointed out that I had been baptized. No longer was I an American tourist, I had become an African resident of Mathare. But I knew that I had a long way to go before I could ever think like one.

Seeing Clearly

➡ MICHAEL demanded that I go to his shoeshine shop so that he could clean my shoes. The shoeshine shop was two walls and an old chair. Michael knelt before me and grabbed my boot. All the sewage that was coated on my foot now covered his jeans. He began with a brush to remove the caked mud from my jeans and boots. Michael, a former street boy, was ministering to me. He cleaned me and all I could give him was a thank you. He took all that he had been given and served me. He gave me back my dignity. Ironically, the same waters that polluted me were the same waters that cleaned me. I was baptized, and what had died was my limited vision and inability to see clearly.

My American prejudice allowed me to see only the filth, disease, and poverty of the neighborhood. I was unable to see that this slum community on the edge of Nairobi was not just a place of lack but also a place of amazing assets. Me and my American money cannot magically solve all the problems in the slums of Nairobi. It's going to take building relationships and community with men like Michael and Moses; taking time to hear what needs to be done to help their community; and then leveraging my resources and connections as an American.

Michael's and Moses' reaction to their community's suffering was not to look away passively or say with resignation, "Oh, what a shame." Their first impulse was to take all they had and to pour all of it back into their community. They look at the world differently than I do. My American individualism is strange to them. Strange and dangerous in a place that needs people to see themselves in relationship to the community they serve and love. Michael, Moses, and the work they do, and the lives they live, speak to this community's profound potential. Michael used his resources to serve me and in doing so revealed to me the power in this community. The power of self-sacrifice and generosity will bring healing and transformation to the community Michael and Moses love. Their power released in the form of servanthood brought healing and transformation to me.

Maybe this is what Paul meant when he challenged the church of Philippi to have the same attitude as Jesus. Jesus, who being in the very nature of God did not regard equality with God something to be grasped, but emptied Himself. New Testament scholar Gordon Fee (*The New International Commentary on the New Testament: Paul's Letter to the Philippians*) says that the text is often misunderstood. Many of us read this passage as implying that Jesus by being human empties Himself of His divinity and power to become human.

Fee says that Paul's intentions are never to minimize the supremacy of Christ. Jesus clearly understands the ways of God. The form of God is something Jesus always was and is. But because of this Jesus realizes that God's way of power isn't grasping or striving. Rather, God pours Himself out for His creation. Jesus pours Himself out because this is the very nature of God. He comes to us and makes Himself of no reputation. This is the essence of God. It's how God loves, serves, and leads in the world.

Fee writes that Jesus understood who God was because Jesus was always with God and is God. Jesus did not regard equality with God something to be grasped. Jesus knew that God was not striving or grasping for power. But the very nature of God is missional, pouring Himself out for humanity and all of creation. So Jesus pours Himself out. Jesus does not empty Himself of anything, but pours Himself out in love for humanity because that is who God is.

The very nature of God is missional, pouring Himself out for humanity and all of creation. So Jesus pours Himself out.

Stanley Saunders and Charles Campbell in *The Word on the Street* say that the humility that is described in this in Philippians 2 is really solidarity with the humiliated. This is a radical call for all of us who serve on the margins. So the question is, what does it mean to have this attitude that Paul speaks of in Philippians?

As I flew to Amsterdam on my way back home, I was humbled by my memories of Michael. I couldn't get out my head the picture of him kneeling before me. I kept thinking about how quickly he took every asset he had at his disposable and poured them out for me. My baptism revealed to me that this young brother, who had the same attitude that Paul encourages the church at Philippi to have, was leading and loving like Jesus.

Moses and Michael are serving in solidarity with the poor in their community, and their first impulse is to serve and to pour themselves out. I was tired, and still a little smelly, but I thanked God for my baptism. In it I was allowed to see the hope for the children of future generations living in Mathare. It is in the men and women of Mathare who, without reservation served me, washed my feet, and revealed to me the attitude of Jesus.

*"For I know that my Redeemer lives,
and at last he will stand upon the earth;
and after my skin has been thus destroyed,
then in my flesh I shall see God,
whom I shall ... behold
and not another."*
—JOB 19:25–27 (NRSV)

12

Even Though You Slay Me

JOB COULD BE ONE OF THE MOST MISUNDERSTOOD MEN IN Scripture. We have all heard the phrase, "He has the patience of Job." This statement implies that the story of Job is about a man learning to understand patience. It implies that Job's story is one of a man's ability to accept delayed gratification, and to be incredibly tolerant of others. However, I think that Job is not about patience; rather it is about incredible suffering. The text poses the question, "Who do we blame for excruciating suffering and what are the purposes of God in the middle of such suffering?" Possibly a more appropriate question is, "Where is God when people suffer?" These themes, all posed in the Book of Job, are themes that haunt the street.

The Scripture claims that Job was a rich man whose heart was true to God. Job was so righteous that he even made sacrifices for his children in case they had sinned. Satan, the enemy of God, believes that it is in an abundance of possessions and good health that Job finds confidence.

Satan goes to God and requests to have access to Job; to put Job to the test; and to see where his faith truly lies. As the story goes on to tell, Job loses everything. He loses his livestock, crops, children, and his own health.

In the middle of this entire calamity, Job has three friends who want to have a theological discussion with him regarding the origins of his suffering and the all-powerfulness of God. Have you ever had a conversation with a friend who wasn't listening to you? You were in crisis, and all they wanted to do was give advice? I think this conversation between Job and his friend was similar to these. The conversation Job had with his friends, like many of our own, ends in frustration and accusations. Even Job's wife encourages him to curse God and die. However, in the end, Job not only keeps faith but truly finds faith in the face of horrendous hardship.

Job's friends symbolize a common understanding of suffering. It's an understanding and view that many hold today—the purpose of suffering is either disciplinary or retributive. God is going to teach you a lesson, or "it's just bad karma." The "powers" are getting you back for something you have done. We see in the story of Job that suffering even touches good people; bad things do happen to very good folks. But the story of Job also reveals that suffering can create something all together different. It creates a place of divine revelation. Suffering puts us in a place to see God in a way that God has not been seen before. Suffering causes Job to humbly admit his ignorance and his confidence in the face of a mysterious God. Job learns that God is in charge, and that he is not.

Falling Out of Community

➡ I find it hard to remember when I first met MIKE. He simply always seemed to be on the street. He was always at New Horizons Ministries' drop-in center.

Early in our friendship I remember going on a camping trip with Mike and having time and opportunity to get to know him better. New Horizons staff members took a bunch of kids out into the woods for a trip into the wild—car camping—as low-key as camping gets. We drove about 35 miles outside the city. We backed the van up and set up camp about 10 yards from someone else, and "lived off the land." We actually lived off the two coolers full of burgers, hot dogs, and marshmallows that sat in the back of the van.

I've been on about 20 camping trips in my years with kids on the street, but this one stands out. These kids were truly urbanized. The thought of living in the woods for three whole days repulsed and terrified most of the kids. "You!" they accused us. "You brought us up here to die or starve, and there are no showers!" The kids, all of them, spent the first 24 hours in the van. Yes, they ate in the van, slept in the van, sat in the van, and the only thing that drew them out of the van was an occasional trip to the sani-can positioned about 30 yards away.

After a full day and night of van confinement, claustrophobia got the best of them. The kids rolled out to throw a Frisbee, and to their surprise, ended up having a great time over the next 48 hours. Mike was one of these kids. I can still see him, probably 14 years old, holding a Frisbee, and stretching out his back after the day and night confined to a sleeping bag draped over a bench seat in the van.

Mike loved sports. We would often catch a baseball game together. He was one of the only kids willing to go inside the dungeon Seattle refers to as "the Kingdome." We also played basketball at some of the downtown parks, and every Wednesday night we played at the downtown YMCA.

Mike's story is pretty typical of a kid ending up on the streets. He was in multiple foster homes—some good, some not so good. His biological mother was seven to eight foster homes removed from his life. His emotional pain, struggles through multiple school systems, and a revolving door of families led him to the streets. With the onset of adolescence, Mike, I'm assuming, looked back and was disappointed in how he had been cared for. As an early adolescent with all its transition, he simply thought he could care for himself.

Like most kids, Mike didn't run to the street; he landed there. A lot of disappointment and pain caused him to fall out of the community. Mike was 11 or 12 when he hit the streets and was on the streets for the next eight or ten years. With life on the street came an addiction to heroin, and also a longing for faith.

Mike always showed up for New Horizons' Sunday night Bible study. While his ability to read was minimal, he never shied away from reading the text aloud. He would always volunteer to read, and with reverence and an indescribable awe, he would slowly read, *"Where can I go from your presence, O Lord?"* or *"For God so loved the world."* At every New Horizons Thanksgiving dinner and every Christmas dinner, Mike was there volunteering to pray in front of the 100 to 200 kids who had gathered to share the holiday meal.

Mike participated in all of New Horizons' Wednesday night recreation activities. In the summer, he participated in softball. He could hit the ball a mile. I can still see his tall, lanky frame trotting out to left field. Usually he had a plate of food in one hand, a mitt in the other, and balanced between the forefinger and the thumb of the glove was a soft drink.

In the fall, he participated in bowling. Mike would find the biggest ball in the alley, roll it with authority down the lane, and as it crashed into the gutter he would laugh, "That's OK; it's not a real sport anyways!" Every winter he'd play basketball. Mike, sometimes loaded on heroin, would barely be able to focus. He would sweat heroin and still dominate.

One cold Wednesday night, we piled into the van, and I tried to get the van running and the heat on as quickly as I could. Just as the fan began to blow warm air, Mike asked, "Could you turn off the heat?" "Turn *off* the heat?" I asked. "Are you sure?" "I'm sure," Mike said with assurance. "I'm on the streets tonight; I don't wanna get warm—it will just mean being colder later on."

I can still see Mike sitting in our outreach office, calling the welfare office, trying desperately to get back into drug treatment. He had been to a 30-day treatment program, a 90-day treatment program, methadone treatment, and Alcoholics Anonymous. This day he was angry, frustrated, and he was crying. He was being told he had been categorized as "not amenable to treatment"; the State would not send him. He had no money, and reality was sinking in. He was stuck with an addiction, and there were no resources to get him healthy. This information was overwhelming. "I am an addict!" he screamed.

I can still see Mike sitting in our outreach office, calling the welfare office, trying desperately to get back into drug treatment.

"I relapsed; of course I am not amenable to treatment, whatever that means. I relapsed. That's why I need treatment so bad!"

Mike's life was a process of two steps forward and one step back. Treatment followed by moments of clarity. This might include a stable place to live, a job, or maybe reuniting with his most recent foster family. This would always be followed by an insatiable desire to feed his addiction. This, in turn, prompted a desperate attempt to find money, which got him heroin, and a trip to jail. This horrible cycle—a revolving door in and out of full-blown addiction, always had moments where Bible study or holiday meals revealed Mike's heart for God. He knew a power greater than himself, and his only hope was that power.

Letting Go

One Wednesday afternoon I was home with my two young sons, while Linda was working at New Horizons. I was hoping for a day where my life and work could feel far away from each other. The phone rang, and it was Linda. "Ron, I have some bad news," she said. "University Hospital just called. Mike is there. He overdosed and is on life support." I immediately thought, *What should I do? Do I subject my own children to the tragedy by going up there and taking them with me? Should I meet Linda at the hospital?* Within minutes I arrived at the Critical Care Unit waiting room—with the kids. Linda was waiting on me and filled me in on a few more details. We sat together with another co-worker and talked through some best guesses on what might have happened.

We knew Mike had been in jail. We also found out that he had been found in an alley in a semi-comatose state as a result of too much heroin. We pieced together that he probably got out of jail, began looking for some drugs, and drank beer to take the edge off his cravings. When he finally found heroin, he didn't factor in the alcohol he had drank. Alcohol, like heroin, is a central nervous system depressant, and jail time often decreases your drug tolerance levels. Mike, thinking that he could handle the same heroin dose as before he was locked up, overdosed. The combination of alcohol and heroin was too much. That's what we guessed. What we knew was, he was barely alive.

The next couple of days were a blur. We were trying to find his biological family, and sitting with Mike in ICU. Late Thursday, Mike's mother was found, and she gave her permission to take him off life support. She was drunk when she called the hospital, and she never came to see her son. She called me and asked if I could be there Friday morning when they took all the breathing machines off her son. She told me her nerves just couldn't handle the stress. When I agreed to be with him, she quickly ended the conversation. It was tragic—her own addiction had severely limited her capacity to care.

Friday morning I went to the hospital and joined my hand to Mike's. The nurse gently touched him as well. She began to unplug, unwrap, and disconnect a myriad of cords and tubes. The only machine left attached was a heart monitor. Mike was dying, his body had been close to this place before, but this time he was losing the gamble with addiction. Two hours went by and I prepared myself for the moment. *What was it like?* I wondered. *Was it like some medical show where a loud beep is followed by a scurry of activity and then silence? Does he rise up and cry out and then pass?* I felt a strange sense of guilt. What was I doing anticipating his death even though it appeared imminent? It felt wrong to try in some way to prepare myself for what I was so unfamiliar with.

Another hour slowly went by. A dear friend and volunteer from New Horizons stopped by. She gently combed Mike's hair as his breathing became shallow and then normal again. Sonja always seemed to be able to see the best in kids, and like a big sister she sat filled with grace as she gently cared for Mike. A few more hours passed and Sonja left. I had now sat with Mike about six hours. He kept going. A nurse commented on his strength. I began to hope. Maybe God was doing a miracle. Maybe God was going to raise Mike up. This would bear witness to the power of God. He would be free, delivered, and the miracles would all be attributed to God; nothing else could save him. Linda stopped by the hospital. She, like only a lifelong partner can, told me it was time to leave. I walked away from his bed imagining *what if; what if he makes it?!*

Saturday morning I decided to stay home. The hospital had my number, and I had two little boys who needed Dad at their little league games. It was hard, but the distance was good. It caused me to do less figuring out and more praying. That entire week a psalm played through my head. On Saturday I couldn't escape it. I heard it over and over— a version of Psalm 143 put to music by a friend of mine. I prayed it in all the quiet moments between Wednesday and Saturday. *"Oh Lord, hear my prayer, hear my cry for mercy. Come to my relief. Hear my cry for mercy."*

Sunday morning my family was running late for church, but before we had time to dash out the door, the phone rang. It was a nurse. She politely asked if I was the "minister" from New Horizons. I explained who I was and that I had been up to the hospital a lot that week. She told me Mike was doing poorly, and his sister had asked that a chaplain from New Horizons come up and pray for him. Immediately, I was out the door and on my way to the hospital. When I arrived in his room, he was struggling. His breathing was short and inconsistent; his foster sister lay next to him. He was dying. His body was shutting down, and the smell of a person trapped in a coma unable to defecate filled the room. Yes, he was dying.

"He is waiting for you," his sister cried. "He's waiting for you to pray." I tried to comfort her. "No, he's not," I replied. "You're doing a great job of comforting him." "No," she exclaimed. "He wants to be with God. Pray for him so he can go!"

I wrapped my arms around Mike's head, his body lay motionless, his eyes open but unresponsive. Psalm 143— *"Oh Lord, hear Mike's prayer, hear his cry for mercy, come to his relief."* It was the only thing that seemed to fit.

He looked a long ways away. He breathed his last breath and was gone. All those years seemed to culminate in this moment. After all the pain, relapse, and laughter, he was gone. I felt a lot in that short half-hour. Feelings that really only compare to the birth of my two sons. I had been given a gift. Mike's sister was far more spiritually aware than I was. She knew what I now realize. I had watched Mike be born again—ushered into a new kingdom.

Letting God In

We could probably debate the righteousness of Mike's life. He sure wasn't rich—most of the time he didn't have an extra pair of socks. The writer of Job seemed to connect Job's lack of sin in the middle of his suffering with his unwillingness to blame God for the injustice that had befallen him. I can see a parallel with Mike.

Mike once participated in an art night at New Horizons. We

"The black part is empty. It's my addiction. The white part represents the places I have let God in.

made masks by taking plaster, placing it in on our faces, and removing it. Once the plaster had hardened it was removed from our faces, we painted the masks, and told what the masks represented for each of us. Mike's mask was two-sided. One of the sides was black; one was white, divided in the middle by his nose. The white side was covered with what from a distance looked liked glitter.

As I moved closer to the mask I could tell it was created like a broken mirror. Numerous pieces of glass had been glued onto the white backdrop. "The black part is empty. It's my addiction. It's my life without God. It's nothing," Mike said. "The white part—it might look broken, but it represents the places I have let God in. He knows me, and because He knows me, I'm clean." Like Job, Mike never could be accused of blaming God for his struggle with heroin. He knew what he had to own.

At Mike's funeral I was able to reflect on the story of Job. Like Job, Mike knew he was struggling, but he never understood why he was allowed to bear the pain. Why could some people go out and have a beer and not watch their lives spiral out of control? Other people could go to treatment, addicted to heroin, and come out of it never using again. Not Mike. He tried repeatedly. Like Job, Mike struggled to understand why God didn't end his suffering. In that struggle, Mike confessed his fear, unbelief, and weakness. But like Job, even as "his skin rots" he kept confessing God as faithful and good.

Mike's relentless pursuit of treatment is what the proverb means when it says, "though a righteous man falls seven times, he rises again, but the wicked are brought down by calamity." Mike got up again, over and over. Not because he believed in himself but because of his unwavering belief in God. When the boils of Mike's addiction told him to curse God and die, Mike, like Job, continued to believe. Even on a hospitable bed, his life proclaimed, "if heroin kills my body, I will still believe."

To some people, Mike's life might appear weak and broken. But Mike was at his best when his infirmities made room for the power of God. A God who is powerful even in suffering comforts me. Thomas Merton says, "Power is made perfect in infirmity, and our very helplessness is all the more potent claim on that Divine Mercy who calls to himself, the poor, the little ones, the heavily burdened."

As I hung out with Mike over the years, as I prayed with him when he died, and as I preached his funeral, I was struck by how Job's story came alive when I thought of him. Mike taught me that true destruction occurs when we stop believing. That is when we adhere to the council of Job's wife or our own demons to curse God and die. Great suffering, whether it is a result of our own brokenness or completely out of our control, isn't enough to push God away. In fact, as preacher, and author of *The Good Book Says*, Peter Gomes shares that incredible suffering is a thin place where the human and the divine come in close contact. It is a place where God reveals His mercy, His grace, and His power as very different from the power of this world. This was the power that I was able to bear witness to in Mike's life. A power that was evident at his death. The question that Job and Mike ask you and me is this, "Can our trust in God survive all our brokenness and suffering?"

"We have this hope, a sure and steadfast anchor of the soul, a hope that enters the inner shrine behind the curtain."
—HEBREWS 6:19

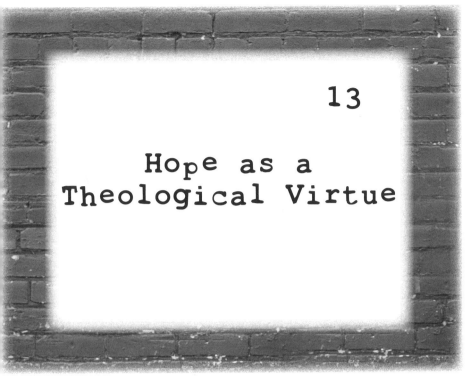

13

Hope as a
Theological Virtue

ONE OF MY FAVORITE MOVIES IS *MEATBALLS*. BILL MURRAY is a camp counselor—one that is a parent's worst nightmare. At the end of the movie, the campers he counsels must participate in Olympic-type games with the camp across the lake. Murray's campers are a skinny, clumsy bunch of kids who exhibit nothing in the way of athletic aptitude. The kids from the other camp look like Greek Olympians. Murray's campers sit in a fireside room anticipating the humiliating defeat of the next day. Murray tries to rally his troops with a few motivating words. He tells them that regardless of the outcome, "It just doesn't matter." After hearing Murray's motivational speech, the group of nerds and outcasts start to chant, "It just doesn't matter. It just doesn't matter." Somewhere in the midst of overwhelming odds, hope is found. Somewhere in the midst of impending doom, hope is realized.

Sometimes those of us who work on the margins of our culture need someone with the perspective of Bill

Murray—someone who can clarify what hope is and what hope is not. Murray's hope overrides an apparently obvious and predictable outcome that seems to be inevitable in everyone's mind. Hope is a strange thing. It dreams of and believes in what is not seen. Hope always sits in a place between what is real and what is longed for. Once something you've hoped for becomes reality, hope is no longer necessary. Hope, like faith, always invests in what is unseen and what is almost unimaginable.

For those on the margins and for those who sit in solidarity with them, there are many things that contribute to feelings of hopelessness. Racism, classicism, poverty, prostitution, prison, overdoses, and murder at times have left me feeling utterly hopeless. What I have seen has given me little reason for hope. Kids on the street die. A Seattle vice officer once told me that he believed half of the young women who enter prostitution as an adolescent die before age 30. The threat of overdose, suicide, murder, and AIDS constantly accompanies the kids we serve. You can't talk about the streets without talking about death. It's a reality that my colleagues and I have to face each day.

At age 21, when I started working with kids on the street, I assumed that my job was to get them off the street and help them understand that they were loved by the Creator of the universe. One of the greatest parts of my job has been the opportunity to not only build friendships with kids but also to help them discover who they were created to be. I've had the incredible privilege of helping them identify their gifts and to see how their circumstances have blinded them to all of their assets and potential.

I never thought I would be an undertaker, and I never thought I would officiate a funeral. But soon after starting to work with kids on the street in Seattle, I pursued clergy credentials. Kids whom I was in relationship with were literally dying, and there were no ordained clergy who knew them well enough to officiate their funerals. While I have been at New Horizons, so many kids have died. When I start to recall the names, I begin to feel hopeless.

➡ ELLEN was stabbed to death on a cold night in front of an adult entertainment center. We had made plans to attend a minor league hockey game the following week. In the early 1980s she was the queen bee on the streets.

➡ WAYNE hung himself in juvenile detention the night before his 17th birthday. His was the first memorial service I attended on the streets. His death was a foreshadowing of all that would come my way.

➡ RANDY died of a heroin overdose. My last memory of him was watching him in New Horizons' drop-in center, eating more corndogs than I thought was humanly possible. He cried one day when he thought he was HIV positive then laughed at his paranoia a week later when he got his test results. Negative!! He beat death by AIDS only to be killed by heroin.

➡ SHANE had severe alcohol problems and fell drunk into the street. He was hit by a car and never made it to the hospital.

➡ CEDRIC was shot, leaving the home of a woman he had allegedly sexually assaulted. Not even the other street kids would come to his funeral. He died alone and was buried by a few New Horizons staff members.

➡ BARRY was shot in the head trying to steal from a drug dealer.

➡ MARY died of AIDS. She was preceded in death by her oldest daughter who also died of AIDS. I sat next to her ten-year-old daughter at the funeral. What do you say to a little girl whose mother and sister have just died, and whose father, also plagued with AIDS, will probably be next?

➡ **FRED** just kept getting skinnier and skinnier. Linda and I took him out for fish and chips for lunch. A few weeks later we heard he had died in a motel room.

➡ **KARLA** was part of the crowd of young people on the streets who were being destroyed by HIV- and AIDS-related illnesses. She, too, died with the same fate. She was a young woman who laughed her way through life. Her mischievous smile got her whatever she needed. She died like she lived, with a smile and with grace.

➡ **BOB** was a red-haired, freckled-faced boy from eastern Washington. He also contracted HIV and was committed to a mental hospital where he died of lung cancer. He was one of those young people who always kept in contact with me through collect calls. When he abruptly stopped calling, I didn't have to ask, I knew that we had lost him.

➡ **DEAN** was the biggest skinhead I had ever seen. He would come in my office, just to talk and have someone listen to him. He was killed in an alcohol-related car accident.

➡ **CHICKEN**, the nicest kid you could ever meet, played basketball and had a great Mohawk haircut. He died in a fight, and his assailants were never brought to justice.

➡ **JAY** died alone in his new apartment. He was making it when addiction reared its ugly head again. He overdosed. He was so close.

➡ **JOHNNY** died in King County jail. He had a blood clot or a stroke or something else. No one knows.

➡ **SAM** was hanging out with friends when he was hit by a train. He was a gentle, loving kid who was the life of the party and a light in our drop-in center.

➡ **JENNA** died of an overdose the night before she was scheduled to be admitted to an inpatient drug rehabilitation program. We have a photo of her standing on New Horizons' porch, suitcase at her feet, her baby in her arms. She too was so close.

One year, the staff at New Horizons participated in 15 funerals and memorial services for kids we knew and loved. Much of what we see on the street can lead to hopelessness and despair. As I've said, every year about 1,500 kids visit the drop-in center in Seattle. Many of the young women struggle in isolation with unplanned pregnancies; many young men run at the very thought of premature fatherhood. This means that without some miracle, they will pass on the baton of abuse, neglect, and rejection to another generation. Nights in emergency rooms with kids who've gambled with addiction and lost tell us overdose leads to death; it's only a matter of time.

One year, the staff at New Horizons participated in 15 funerals and memorial services for kids we knew and loved.

Hope in Disguise

There are many reasons for us to take a blanket of despair and cover ourselves, hoping to hide from what appears to be the inevitable, hopeless outcome for the kids we serve. Cornelius Plantinga, in *Not the Way It's Supposed to Be,* speaks of the brokenness in this world. He says, "The story of the fall tells us that sin corrupts: It puts asunder what God has joined together and joins together what God has put asunder. Like some devastating twister, corruption both explodes and implodes creation, pushing it back toward the 'formless void' from which it came."

The diabolical nature of evil is that it literally pulls apart our lives. This is true for those of us who live on and off the streets. For those on the street, their lives have been thrown into a formless void. Societal, family, and individual corruption has caused their souls to drift aimlessly; without direction; without limits; and most importantly, without hope. When serving these forgotten and abandoned young people with all that they face, there's plenty to be hopeless about.

So much that we see could lead us into deep despair, but there is hope. It is truly a theological virtue, and its definition should have an impact on the way Christians live, and how we see kids who survive on the streets. The hope of the Old Testament calls us to look back. In the story of the Exodus, and the crossing of the Red Sea, God faithfully rescues the Hebrew people. Their history is now defined by that moment. Hope pushes us forward. It is the story of Jeremiah, an Old Testament prophet who buys land in a country that was no longer his own. He knew that his future was in the hands of God.

There is no better example of hope than that of Jesus' interaction with people pushed to the margins. As Jesus came in contact with lepers, women, children, the blind, and the poor, the interaction always ended in hope. It is in these interactions that Jesus built community, and the people around Him discovered hope. He was able to speak to their pain, while simultaneously speaking to a future they could not see. A woman came in shame to a well in the middle of the day. She later became Jesus' missionary to the Samaritans. The same woman, who was all alone at the well, told an entire community about Jesus. A demon-possessed man was delivered and left to bear witness to the same neighbors who had pushed him into the cemetery. A blind man claimed that he was no Pharisee; all he knew was that he was blind and then he could see.

A Simple Touch

There is nothing more hopeless in Scripture than the plight of the leper. More than a medical problem, it was a social disease of the first century. The community that surrounded the leper ostracized him. I have heard it said that rabbis in the time of Jesus would boast that they wouldn't even buy fruit from a market that faced a street where a leper had walked. Lepers stood on the fringe of society, yelling a warning to the world around them, "Stay away; I'm unclean." In Luke's Gospel, there are many stories of such lepers.

> *"Once, when he was in one of the cities, there was a man covered with leprosy. When he saw Jesus, he bowed with his face to the ground and begged him, 'Lord, if you choose you can make me clean.' Then Jesus stretched out his hand, touched him, and said, "I do choose. Be made clean" (Luke 5:12–13).*

I have an incredible life, a great wife, a warm home, and two wonderful sons. They will scold me for saying this, but much of what I have hoped for is displayed in who my sons are becoming. They are better at the things I love than I am. Ben is completing a degree in sociology, serving kids in our neighborhood, and he's a great athlete. He uses his love of sports to invite kids into his work and his life. Clayton is a rock-and-roll musician and a poet. He speaks and sings and people listen. Even at a young age he is not afraid to speak truth to power. Many rainy nights, I sit in front of a fire and sincerely believe I am the richest man on the planet. I'm sure many men throughout history have had the same feelings.

I can only imagine what it must have been like to contract leprosy. It may have gone something like this:

One normal morning I wake up and as I dress I notice a small bruise on my bicep. I think nothing of it until a few days pass and the bruise-like abrasions are spreading. In a little bit of panic I decide to wear long sleeves to work. But nothing can hide the inevitable outcome. One evening as I sit with my family I hear a knock at the front door. It's my family's rabbi. "Ron," he says. "They've been talking down at the synagogue. We think you have leprosy." As I roll up my sleeves he tells me what I already know. That night I leave my home. Never again will I feel my wife's touch. Never again will I hear my sons' laughter around the dinner table. Forever, I am cast out of my community. I have no more family. I have no more friends. I'm not just physically sick—I'm labeled dirty, unclean, sinful. I spend the remainder of my life warning anyone who comes close to me. "Stay away I'm unclean!"

I can't imagine what it must have felt like to see Jesus. Maybe I had heard about Him, some holy man, a miracle-working teacher. I lose control when I see Him. I'm so desperate to be healed that I forget the rules. I give Him no warning. I run toward Him, telling Him what He already knows. If He is willing, He can make me clean. He could have healed me by speaking or make some sort of gesture in the air, but for some reason He chooses to touch me. My first touch since I left my home so long ago.

Of course, I'm only imagining; I can't really know what it was like. However, I think it's easy for us to forget that the leper mentioned in Luke's Gospel is someone who has been ostracized. Jesus is probably the first person to touch him since he was banished from his community. Sometimes I wonder what the bigger sign of hope in this story was: the miracle of the healing, or the willingness of Jesus to simply touch someone labeled dirty, unclean, defiled.

At Heaven's Door

➡ The phone in my office rings constantly. Picking up the receiver is second nature. I grab it without thinking. One day I picked up the phone and I heard a familiar voice belt out, "Accept the charges, Ronnie." Then, "Would you accept a collect call from JAMES?" the operator asked. James was in the State prison and collect phone calls were his connection with the outside world. As I began to ask James how he was doing, he told me he was "Dead!" I thought, *James, what did you do? Did you buy dope, borrow money? How did you get into such a mess?* As I began to bombard him with questions, his tone softened and his voice began to break. "I've got AIDS, Ronnie. I'm dead." He called me Ronnie, which lets you in on how long I've known him. My mind began to race. "Are you going to harm yourself?" "No." he replied. "I don't want to die in the joint."

> I began to bombard him with questions, his tone softened and his voice began to break. "I've got AIDS, Ronnie.

James was always excited, and his lethargic tone told me that he was overwhelmed. Definitely not the place you want to leave a guy, depressed and isolated, sitting in a prison cell. "How do I know you are going to be safe?" I asked. James reminded me of a time a few years earlier when he'd been released from another institution. That day, several years prior to the phone call, I had picked him up at the bus depot. I told him that it was his day, and we could do whatever activity he chose to celebrate his release. We ended up at my house eating a pizza, watching a football game, nothing special. He reminded me of this day as we talked on the phone, and I wondered what it had to do with him not killing himself. "Ronnie, if you'll shut up, I'll tell you. I remember that Linda had made hot chocolate. We played with Ben and just hung out. Ronnie," James said, "I want one more day like that before I die." A day that many of us dismiss as a normal Saturday was keeping hope alive.

The last time I saw James, he was downtown in a 280ZX. As he drove away, Bob Dylan's "Knockin' on Heaven's Door" was blasting from his stereo. He was killed in a police chase the following day in that stolen 280ZX. He swapped the sports car for a welfare casket. We soon found out there was no one to bury him and no place to put the casket. After some research, an old girlfriend found an uncle who lived on a reservation across the State. James could be buried there if we were able to transport the body. Myself, a co-worker, James's stepbrothers, his old girlfriend, and a friend from juvenile detention drove his body across the state to the reservation where his uncle lived.

When we arrived at the cemetery, it soon became clear that there was no one to bury James and no one to officiate a graveside service. The only person there was an old man that was there to ring bells and sing as we buried our dead friend and family member. All of us lowered James's body into a six-foot hole on a dusty hill in an eastern Washington cemetery. I buried my friend who just dreamed of a "normal day" before he died.

A few days later I sat early in the morning telling God how unfair the whole thing really was. The most tragic thing about James' death was that the paper told the story of his life in only two paragraphs—a young hood dies trying to outrun police on the interstate. "This was horrible!" I told God. They didn't know him. They didn't know how funny he was, how creative he was, and how his wishes for life were really quite ordinary. The article made it sound like he was known by no one, and he would be missed by no one. As I sat and cried, God reminded me of the gift that I was experiencing. God reminded me that I knew James, and that I would miss him. His life was woven into the fabric of my own. I would be different because of who he was, and I would serve differently because of what he hoped for. The price I paid for knowing him was grieving the loss of him when he was gone.

James taught me a lot about hope. Hope isn't always found in the miraculous, but often in the simplicity of an ordinary day. Hope is given to kids on the street through simple acts of love and kindness. In the end, all James wanted was one more day to hang out with me and my family and eat pizza. That kind of day gave him hope in the middle of an HIV diagnosis.

By inviting young people to our table and asking them to eat with us, hope is given. When New Horizons' staff members take time to kneel before street kids and offer to wash their infected, dirty feet, hope is given. Every time staff members share BBQ with kids on the beach, hope is given. Hope is given when kids experience life-giving friendship in the middle of their chaos. The touch of Jesus is deeply relational and filled with acceptance. It points to something unseen that is much larger than the event. This hope is a foretaste of the kingdom that is to come.

The Greatest of Ironies

In Luke, Jesus touches a leper. Can you imagine the crowd's reaction when Jesus touches him? Jesus was a good Jew. Everyone knew not to touch someone who was unclean. The fear of touching such a filthy, diseased person was that you, too, might end up filthy and diseased. When Jesus touched the man, He chose to take on Himself all that comes with the leprosy—the scorn, the shame, the marginalization.

➡️ **MANY OF OUR YOUNG PEOPLE** experience shame and scorn in life and death. I'm reminded of **ONE YOUNG MAN** in particular who died a horrible death. As my co-workers and I sat in my office trying to plan a memorial service, the tragedy seemed too great. This young man had always kept his distance from the staff. He was like a wounded animal, full of fear. We fed him, clothed him, only to see him run away. He had overdosed and died in a bathhouse. A bathhouse is a place where men seek sexual gratification without intimacy. They drift from room to room searching for temporary satisfaction. This is a bathhouse at its best. At its worst it's a place where young men sit in small rooms waiting for older men to prey upon them. In return these young men receive a few dollars and a couple hours of sleep. The boy that was in our thoughts had died in such a place. After exchanging sex for drugs or for money, he'd shut the door of his room and shot the memory of what had happened up his arm. He'd shut the door of his room and overdosed on heroin.

As we cried and grieved this young man's passing, our impulse was to turn away, to look elsewhere for some glimmer of hope. I remember praying something like, "God help me to see something else besides the image of this bathhouse." The image of **DANNY** dying alone was too much to bear. I sat in silence, and then these words came:

You cannot lift your eyes from the revolting image of a bathhouse to gaze into the eyes of Christ.

If your hope is in the looking away, you really have no hope at all, but a mere fantasy of the world in which we live.

In looking into a bathhouse and seeing the broken body of a young boy destroyed by the meanness of this world, hope still must be found.

It is the greatest of ironies. It is in the filth, the shame, the abandonment—that Christ can be found and hope is realized.

Don't turn away.
Look at the boy.
A boy forsaken.
There you will see our Lord,
Forsaken for the boy.
Forsaken with the boy.

Despair is a luxury that claims we can all give up. Despair claims that nothing about today has impact on tomorrow. Despair asks, "Why would you grieve for an addict who overdoses on heroin? Why would you be on the street with kids who don't seem to want you there? Why would you visit kids in jail who have participated in a horrible crime? Why would you open a drop-in center for young people who claim to have no interest in finding housing or receiving services?" Despair is a temporal value, but hope is an eternal value.

This is the hope of the gospel, that in our sin and isolation we find Christ with us.

The hope of the gospel is that in the midst of leprosy, AIDS, or being abandoned on the street, hope is revealed by God's simple touch. We can also reveal God's hope by "touching" the wounded places in this world with simple acts of love that proclaim the value of kids who are forgotten on the street.

This is the hope of the gospel, that in our sin and isolation we find Christ with us. He takes upon Himself the desperate state of our humanness on the Cross—and in the bathhouses of this world. God is with us. To be with our young people is to be with Jesus. The question is, does our theology of the Cross penetrate the evil image of the bathhouse? Can hope really be found there?

It always protects, always trusts, always hopes,
always perseveres. Love never fails.
But where there are prophecies, they will cease;
where there are tongues, they will be stilled;
where there is knowledge,
it will pass away.
—1 CORINTHIANS 13:7–8

14

Love Never Ends

EARLY ONE SATURDAY MORNING, I RAN INTO MY FRIEND Lora at a neighborhood coffee shop. She was on her way to the State women's correctional center to visit a young woman she had met on the street during her time as a volunteer at New Horizons.

➡ She had been visiting **AMBER** for 2 years. A decade away from her original New Horizons volunteer commitment, she was still following up with Amber every month, reminding the young woman that she was not forgotten or alone. She wanted Amber to know that there was a "square" lady, a lady with a "normal" life who cared enough to give up a Saturday with her family to visit a young woman in prison.

➡ Another friend, Dave, volunteered at New Horizons more than 25 years ago. We went through the same volunteer training in January 1983. Like Lora, when Dave left New

Horizons as a volunteer, he continued to do follow-up with the young people he had met. He continued to visit a 15-year-old named MACK, who was serving a 6-year sentence in juvenile prison. To this day, Dave and Mack continue to stay in contact. Anytime Mack is in Seattle, he and Dave get together for breakfast.

New Horizons staff and volunteers may move on to other assignments, but New Horizons never really leaves them.

Embarking on a New Journey

Now I am stepping into the unknown, beyond New Horizons, as it's time to allow new leadership to emerge and to let go of the familiar and again welcome change. In August 2009, after 25 years of incredible, life-changing relationships with young people, I resigned from New Horizons Ministries. However, I knew that I would never be able to leave the young people I'd known, completely—emotionally or spiritually. The relationships are too deep, and my love for kids on the street is so much a part of who I am. New Horizons will never leave me. The kids are part of who I am.

Now I'm teaching some, training some, but transitioning some too. I've been supporting my incredible wife, Linda, as she became the executive director who launched New Horizons' newly formed partnership business, Street Bean Espresso.

➡ STREET BEAN ESPRESSO opened in November 2009, to provide formerly homeless or street-involved young people with job training and employment, equipping them with skills necessary to exit street life.

However, the Street Bean vision took years to form. It was born out of the hopes and prayers of volunteers and staff over New Horizons' 30-year history. The vision was birthed through people who know firsthand that employment is a key component in empowering young people to exit street life.

➡ RITA NUSSLI, the former executive director of New Horizons Ministries, made the creation of a business a priority in the New Horizons organization's overall strategic planning. In 2006, a planning committee comprised of New Horizons Ministries paid staff, board members, volunteers, donors, and community members was established.

➡ DAVE HUNT, a New Horizons volunteer, led the committee that deliberated for 12 months about the kind of business to start. Some of the ideas included a hair salon, dog walking service, secondhand clothing store, scrap metal salvage, and window washing business.

Dog walking seemed to be one of the best prospects. It required low overhead and met a real service need in a neighborhood that was expanding with condo ownership. However, the unthinkable disaster of losing someone's dog seemed too much to risk.

Scrap metal salvage also seemed to have great potential. All that would have been needed was a truck. However, scrap salvage did not meet the planning committee's criteria that the business have equal appeal to young men and young women. Neither would it have served as a launching pad to introduce young people to an industry of people that could potentially hire them.

➡ THE PLANNING COMMITTEE prayed and thought carefully about what would provide the best strategy to prepare and equip kids not only for possibly their first job but also for their perceptions of their future.

After months of deliberating, New Horizons finally decided to open the coffee shop. Part of our decision hinged on the fact that a supporter who had extensive experience in the industry was willing to consult with us on the project. However, even with his support, coffee is a very competitive business in the Seattle area. Even so, we felt like it would provide both young men and young women with good employment skills and opportunities.

Miraculously, a great location for the café was available right across from New Horizons' drop-in center! At the same time our discernment process was going on, our neighbor was preparing to lease a portion of his building space. He was enthusiastic about supporting the new business venture and offered Street Bean Espresso a year of free rent. With this generous support from our new landlord, the New Horizons board of directors took a leap of faith and endorsed moving forward with the coffee shop and the business plan.

In any economy there's always risk starting up a new business; however, at that time, with the economy in particular dire straights, the creation of a new business entailed even greater risk. Linda became project manager, and after two years of fundraising, planning, and God's leading and grace, Street Bean launched. Linda has been overseeing the business as its executive director.

Street Bean is located in the Belltown neighborhood of Seattle. The business provides young people, who were formally on the street, an opportunity to work for up to two years. Through Street Bean's partnering roaster, Caffe Lusso Coffee Roasters, the café serves a delicious cup of coffee. It also offers free Wi-Fi and has become a community gathering place for the Belltown neighborhood. The business is beautifully designed and local residents are using the space as an extension of their living rooms, while local businesses are using the community meeting room as an extension of their offices. If you were to walk into Street Bean, you would see local real estate agents, condo owners, New Horizons staff and the young people they serve, all drinking coffee together. You would also see the artwork of local artists on the walls and pounds of coffee being sold, providing farmers a fair and just wage.

This must have been what Paul saw when he walked into Corinth—the crossroads of the first-century world. It is a perfect place to engage in conversation across gender, ethnic, and economic lines. Crossing barriers is the power of the message of good news brought by Jesus.

Helping People

Street Bean is reclaiming and sustaining the lives of young people at New Horizons through meaningful employment. Street Bean is also helping to reclaim and sustain the lives of coffee farmers through the relationally driven purchasing practices of Caffe Lusso Coffee Roasters. N. T. Wright in his book *Surprised by Hope* describes the coming of God's kingdom by three significant attributes: justice, evangelism, and beauty. I see all of these attributes being exemplified at Street Bean Espresso. The walls that divide people are coming down and a strong community is being built. This good news of reconciliation in God's kingdom—justice, evangelism, and beauty—is beginning to work itself out in this gateway place known as the Street Beans community.

The walls that divide people are coming down and a strong community is being built... good news of reconciliation in God's kingdom— justice, evangelism, and beauty.

Young people in Seattle who once survived on the streets are now selling a great cup of coffee from beans grown by farmers from some of the poorest places in the world.

Farmers are growing good beans that are being bought at a fair price, and are giving young people a chance to develop a work history.

Local artists have a venue to display and sell their paintings, and

small business owners have a conference room.

Street Bean Espresso is bringing together a community of condo owners, street kids, and farmers. But first, it was just a new construction site.

➡ ONE KID, had spent the day demolishing a wall, serving community service hours for his probation. The next night during his drop-in, he told the outreach staff about his six-hour demolition project.

"Someday when I have kids, I am going to bring them to Street Bean and show them what I worked on." I don't think he has ever read Joshua, heard of the crossing, or been introduced to the memorial, but he was acting it out.

Making It Through Your First Job

Being able to accept intense supervision from an authority figure can be a challenge. I vividly remember my first job. I was hired to work at a 24-hour café. On my first (only) night, my co-worker, who thought he was an expert dish-washer, decided to teach me how to manage the 2:00 A.M. bar rush. He yelled at me, and I left! I lasted on that job for less than an evening—three hours to be exact. At age 16, I couldn't separate the job—the tasks required of me and the intense supervision—from me as a person. I took it all personally. I had no idea how to work and how to be myself on a job that seemed to disrespect me and challenge who I thought I was. These are adaptive life skills that some people acquire through their families, and others seem to obtain naturally through some sort of osmosis-like process. However, for many of us, these are skills that we need to learn and have modeled for us come from outside the family.

➡ When MY SONS were small, I remember trying to mow my lawn—with one of them in a backpack. As Ben and Clayton grew, each of them would play beside me, mimicking my work with a plastic lawn mower. I would mow, and they would run alongside me. The day came when they wanted to push the lawn mower themselves, and ever so slowly, they began to mow the lawn. They both grew stronger, and soon they were yanking the cord.

Last summer, Ben, my oldest son, was home from college. One particular Sunday afternoon, Linda and I took a walk, but knowing that the lawn needed mowing kept me distracted. As we turned the corner, approaching our house, I could see that Ben had positioned himself on a blanket and was soaking up the summer sun. As I got a little closer I also noticed that the grass looked great. I looked at Ben and asked him what happened.

He answered matter-of-factly, "Oh, the lawn looked like it needed cutting, so I did it before lying out in the sun." My sons learned to work and to take initiative from two parents and a caring community. It was a longterm organic process, one that kids in hard places rarely get to experience.

Sometimes we wonder who is helping who, and maybe that is how it should be. On Street Bean's first day, one of the new employees showed up for work at 4:30 A.M. because she was afraid that the 5:00 A.M. bus would cut it too close, and she didn't want to be late for work. Street Bean initially hired five young people. They were all crossing their own rivers, making transitions, remembering where they came from, and making choices of where they're heading to now.

Sure, this new venture is not without its challenges. As the young people experience the safety of job security and housing, hard things boil to the surface. The young people have had to take a hard look at what has kept them on the streets. They have to be on time and hear the truth about job skills and customer service. They are challenged with many barriers when it comes to getting and keeping employment, but every day they are coming back. Linda told them that if they were to thrive in the world of employment, they would have to be willing to hear the truth about these barriers and their performance. She told them at Street Bean they would all have to hear and speak truth in love. As one of the baristas struggled to perfect a macchiato, Linda sensitively began to critique her technique. But the young woman blurted out, "Linda, I know you love me, it's OK to tell me the truth, the truth in love!"

It is hard to tell the story of Street Bean without mentioning the young people who work there. They represent all the other kids on the street who haven't made it off yet. They have a huge responsibility to their peers when all they wanted was a job, a little anonymity, and off the street. They are taking a courageous journey for themselves and the other kids.

Young people on the streets can not only teach us to remember, but they teach us *how to remember*. As we cross our own rivers, we must remember our own pain and how God helped us face it, and then encouraged us to move on. We must also remember that God's ways of salvation and deliverance are as unique as the people God delivers. Each of us has our own story and our own river. These stories, when remembered, can liberate people in exile.

➡ Already we are seeing a new phase of miracles. THE YOUNG BARISTAS build coffee drinks without fear or insecurity. It's like a 19-year-old and a 48-year-old learning a foreign language. The 19-year-old jumps into the new world where the older adult cautiously moves forward. The young people are up to the challenge. They are making drinks, taking risks, and learning the new world of coffee. On several occasions, they have initiated passing out flyers in the neighborhood.

Coming from the streets, the young people employed at Street Bean are keenly aware of their surroundings. This is a great asset in a busy coffee shop where a lot of things are happening at once. Oh, they get frustrated and often bored during slow business times, but they are all moving forward, and their ability to be streetwise has become an asset in the coffee shop.

We must remember that God's ways of salvation and deliverance are as unique as the people God delivers.

After the first month, Linda posted a sign in the break room congratulating the two young people who had perfect attendance. I signed the poster, "I am so proud!! Dr. Ron." One barista who has been late a time or two looked at the sign and declared, "I will not be late next month. I want you to be proud of me!" I assured her that I was still proud of her, even if she didn't have perfect attendance and that, when she did have perfect attendance, I'd have one more thing to commend her on.

During a slow time one morning, one of the baristas was totaling the monthly sales receipts. When I asked her what she was doing, she told me that she was tracking sales so that Linda could have an idea of how the coffee shop was doing in the first month. A while later she told me with uncharacteristic excitement that sales were going up each week!

On another day, Linda arrived at Street Bean at 5:30 A.M. to find out that the local delivery service who was supposed to deliver coffee the previous evening had mistakenly rerouted the order. It looked like she would surely run out of coffee before the morning was over. Not knowing who to call at 5:30 A.M., Linda thought she might have to close for an hour in order to get more coffee. However, the young person working that morning assured her that he could run the shop just fine while she was gone. Linda left him in charge, and an hour later, returned to see everything running smoothly.

After four years of planning and preparation, Street Bean is taking shape. It might not become the shape we all thought originally. We all have thought it to be the next step to job readiness, and to be self-sustaining. What it appears to be becoming is one more deeply sensitive connection for isolated kids to find belonging. It isn't just about a job; it is moving kids from the isolation of street life into relationship and towards community. Street Beans is a public business that gives kids a chance to create another place of relationship and family, of belonging. Jobs are important but being known and knowing others is lifesaving. Street Bean is giving kids a chance to give and receive in the greater community.

The Least of These

It says in Matthew's Gospel that what we have done to the least of these we have done to Jesus.

During my last week at New Horizons, I walked through the drop-in center to say goodbye to the kids who were eating breakfast.

➡ LACEY, a young girl, asked me, "Dr. Ron, what is sin?" I laughed and said, "Sin is like bacon. It tastes as good as it is bad for you!" We both laughed, and then she looked at me in all seriousness and said, "No it's not. That might be what they say in church, but that isn't sin." She was right, and as we talked more she said that sin is a human condition, a place where we get stuck. She knew that sinful behaviors are a by-product of a place of paralysis that we can't change on our own. We laughed about the bacon and she encouraged me that it was funny, but she also pointed out that it was a bad analogy. The kids may be on the street, but they are smart.

From the day I first walked the streets of Seattle until the day I walked through New Horizons' drop-in center to say goodbye to the kids, one thing has remained constant—the love God gave me for each one never subsided. By God's beautiful grace He sustained me, and I never "burned out" on the kids. I loved being with them and loved the privilege of serving them. I learned that they were not a problem to be solved or a group of people to convert. They were young people in pain. Some would lash out because of their brokenness, some would keep their distance, while others would open up too much too quickly—desperately wanting someone to listen. But all of these young people who have been labeled "the least of these" have been my most profound teachers.

They have taught me these lessons that I take with me on all the stages of this life's journey into the next:

- Regardless of who runs out on you, Jesus doesn't forsake you.
- I have learned that the delivery of that message must be tangible and practical, often requiring it to take the shape of a father running to meet a

son who squandered his family's legacy. It has to be incarnational—love with skin on it.

- As I have supported kids in walking away from the streets, I have learned that their ability to move beyond the damage of their wounded families and the meanness of the streets is most effectively addressed when they are able to remember the tragedy of their past, rather than forget it.

- I have also learned that my ability to serve and to help is directly connected to my ability to remember my own pain and history and how it impacts who I am. Our then and there is always mixed up with our here and now until we take the journey back to the painful reality of how our history and our pain have shaped us.

- I have learned that to serve young people on the streets we must have a community that refuses to believe the voice of a dominant culture that says these kids are nothing, never have been, and never will be. It takes a community of people to stand alongside these kids and say no to this message of sinful exclusion—exclusion that tosses them among the dead. We must say no to exclusion that pushes young people to the margins of our community so they won't be a reminder of our community's brokenness and our inability to fix them or ourselves.

- It also takes a community to set a table, like the many tables in Luke's Gospel where all are welcome and no one's hands are too dirty to eat. It is at this table that you begin to discover that we are all created in the image and likeness of God.

We must all do things to breathe life into that awareness. Street Bean Espresso will not survive without a community of people who are willing to come to the table; individuals who will intentionally support this business because they believe the kids are worth it.

It does take a community to heal these kids, but it is not a community of good people helping bad people. It is all of us working together to tell the whole story of God. Each of us has blind spots, "logs in our eyes," that are removed when we walk together. Teaching and learning are discovered in relationships where we recognize that all of us have something to learn and give. I didn't need to go to Guatemala or Kenya to learn this, but that is where I discovered it. In places so different from my comfort zone, I was able to see a God who is different from me. Transcendence, the otherness of God, is revealed through diverse communities and diverse relationships that together tell the whole story of God.

I have seen faith in action in the young people on the streets. Mike, who lost his struggle against addiction, taught me that faith is simply a trusting allegiance to Jesus. As Mike struggled with addiction and died as a result, he had no faith in himself. He had no false pretense that would cause him to trust in his own abilities. But he

Death did not separate him. Death did not destroy him. Hope is the belief that the Resurrection is the final word on our destiny.

believed Jesus could save him. Even through the surety of death, Mike had faith in Jesus. The resurrection of Jesus meant that even when Mike died, death did not separate him. Death did not destroy him. Hope is the belief that the Resurrection is the final word on our destiny. Jesus' words to us are, "Go, you are forgiven." Jesus' words to us are that through His death and resurrection He makes all things new. Hope, disguised.

There is no way to tie up the lives of kids on the streets into some tidy theological bow. I can't create some linear step-by-step approach that will insure that, when you meet a young person, you can lead him or her straight into the American dream.

However, I can say this:

➡ Jesus said, when we have acted toward THE LEAST OF THESE, we have done whatever we have done unto Him. Yet, not because the least are a problem to be solved, but because they reveal the brokenness and the faith found in all of us. They reveal US to ourselves and, in some strange way, they reveal the flesh and blood of Jesus among us— who loves us, heals us, and asks us to bear witness to a good God who wants to tell the world it's loved. I guess if you walk down almost any street, you might walk past the least of these. I encourage you to not walk past them or to ignore them, as uncomfortable or painful as that might be. They have the potential to be your greatest teachers. When you see them, you see **JESUS**.

Bibliographies

In gathering these bibliographies, it's obvious that this includes many available resources—and includes a few Web sites you can visit—however, others are available beyond this. To all those incredible authors whose works I have yet to read and acknowledge, I look forward to learning from you.

Here you will find a type of "greatest hits" that have accompanied my learning process. This is what I do know: to serve the world that continues to urbanize and globalize, ministry practitioners' knowledge-base must be as eclectic and diverse as the contexts in which we find ourselves.

Regularly, I instruct students that effective urban ministry practitioners serving youth and families must be a unique blend of competencies and dimensions:

- a solid cup of theologian,
- one part sociologist,
- about two parts chaplain, and a pinch of social worker,
- a bunch of community organizer, and
- add a little of an anthropologist.

One must be able to use the *context* as a classroom and take clues from one's context in order to serve *in that context* effectively.

I hope these resources reflect what has had a positive impact on my thinking as I have been serving youth and families in hard places.

Theology of Missions

Abraham, William J. *The Logic of Evangelism*. Grand Rapids, MI: Eerdmans, 1989.

Bosch, David, J. *Transforming Mission: Paradigm Shifts in Theology of Mission*. New York: Orbis, 1991.

Brueggemann, Walter. *The Prophetic Imagination*. Minneapolis: Fortress, 1978.

_____. *An Introduction to the Old Testament: The Canon and Christian Imagination*. Louisville, KY: Westminister John Knox Press, 2003.

Byrne, Brendan. *The Hospitality of God: A Reading of Luke's Gospel*. Collegeville, MI: The Liturgical Press, 2000.

Fee, Gordon. *Paul, the Spirit, and the People of God*. Peabody, MA: Hendrickson Publishing, 1996.

Gomes, Peter, J. *The Good Book: Reading the Bible With the Mind and Heart*. New York: William Morrow, 1996.

Green, Joel B., and Mark D. Baker. *Recovering the Scandal of the Cross: Atonement in the New Testament and Contemporary Contexts*. Downers Grove, IL: IVP Academic, 2000.

Hauerwas, Stanley, and William H. Wilimon. *Resident Aliens: Life in the Christian Colony.* Nashville: Abingdon, 1989.

Moltmann, Jurgen. *The Crucified God.* Minneapolis: Fortress Press, 1993.

Newbigin, Lesslie. *The Gospel in a Pluralistic Society.* Grand Rapids, MI: Eerdmans, 1989.

Wainwright, Geoffrey. *Lesslie Newbegin: A Theological Life.* New York: Oxford, 2000.

Wallis, Jim. *The Call to Conversion: Recovering the Gospel for These Times.* New York: Harper Publishing Company, 1988.

Wright, N. T. *The New Testame:nt and the People of God.* Minneapolis: Fortress Press, 1992.

_____. *Surprised by Hope: Rethinking Heaven, The Resurrection, and the Mission of the Church.* New York: Harper One, 2008.

Adolescents

Brendtro, Larry, and Scott Larson. *Reclaiming Our Prodigal Sons and Daughters: A Practical Approach for Connecting with Youth in Conflict*. Bloomington, IN: National Education Service, 2000.

Diapolo, Micheal. *The Impact of Multiple Childhood Trauma on Homeless Runaway Adolescents*. New York: Garland Publishing Inc., 1999.

Elkind, David. *All Grown Up and No Place to Go*. Reading, MA: Addison-Wesley, 1984.

Finnegan, William. *Cold New World: Growing Up in a Harder America*. New York: The Modern Library, 1999.

Garbarino, James. *Raising Children in a Socially Toxic Environment*. San Francisco: Jossey Bass Books, 1995.

_____. *Lost Boys: Why Our Sons Turn Violent and How to SaveThem*. New York: First Anchor Books, 1999.

Gil, Eliana. *Treating Abused Adolescents*. New York: Gilford Press, 1996.

Hersch, Patricia. *A Tribe Apart: A Journey into the Heart of America Adolescence*. New York: Ballantine Books, 1998.

Howard, Gary R. *We Can't Teach What We Don't Know: White Teachers, Multiracial Schools*. New York: Teachers College Press, 1999.

Janus, Mark-David. *Adolescent Runaways: Causes and Consequences.* New York: Lexington Books, 1987.

Klein, Malcolm, W. *The American Street Gang: Its' Nature, Prevalence, and Control.* New York: Oxford Press, 1995.

Kitwana, Bakari. *The Hip Hop Generation: Young Blacks and the Crisis in the African American Culture.* New York: Basic Books, 2002.

Kindlon, Dan, PhD, and Michael Thompson, PhD, *Raising Cain: Protecting the Emotional Life of Boys.* New York: Ballantine Books, 2000.

Kozol, Jonathan. *Amazing Grace: Lives of Children and the Conscience of a Nation.* New York: Crown Publishing, 1996.

Muss, Rolf. *Theories of Adolescence.* New York: McGraw Hill Publishing, 1996.

Pipher, Mary. *Reviving Ophelia: Saving the Selves of Adolescent Girls.* NewYork: Grosset/Putnam Book, 1994.

Pollack, William, PhD, *Real Boys: Rescuing Our Sons from the Myths of Boyhood.* New York: Henry Holt, 1996.

Ponton, Lynn, E., MD. *The Romance of Risk: Why Teenagers Do the Things They Do.* New York: Basic Books, 1997.

Postman, Neil. *The Disappearance of Childhood*. New York: Vintage Books, 1982.

Toth, Jennifer. *Orphans of the Living: Stories of America's Children in Foster Care*. New York: Simon & Shuster, 1998.

Urban Ministry and Social Justice

Anderson, Elijah. *Street Wise: Race, Class and Change in an Urban Community*. Chicago: University of Chicago Press, 1990.

Bakke, Ray. *A Theology as Big as the City*. Downers Grove, IL: Intervarsity Press, 1997.

Burns, Edward, and Simon, David. *The Corner: A Year in the Life of an Inner City Neighborhood*. New York: Broadway Books, 2000.

Conn, Harvey, and Manuel Ortiz. *Urban Ministry: The Kingdom, the City, and the People of God*. Downers Grove, IL: Intervarsity Press, 2001.

De La Torre, Miguel A. *Reading the Bible from the Margins*. New York: Orbis, 2002.

Dyson, Michael, Eric. *Race Rules: Navigating the Color Line*. New York: Vintage Books, 1996.

_____. *Holler If You Hear Me: Searching for Tupac Shakur*. New York: Basic Books, 2001.

Ekblad, Bob. *Reading the Bible with the Damned*. Louisville, KY: John Knox, 2005.

Emerson, Michael, and Christian Smith. *Divided by Faith: Evangelical Religion and the Problem of Race in America*: New York: Oxford, 1999.

Green, Clifford J. Joel, ed. *Churches, Cities and Human Community: Urban Ministry in the United States 1945–1985*. Grand Rapids, MI: Eerdmans, 1996.

Katz, Michael B. *The Undeserving Poor: From the War on Poverty to the War on Welfare*. New York: Pantheon Books, 1989.

Law, Eric H. F. *The Wolf Shall Dwell with the Lamb: A Spirituality for Leadership in a Multicultural Community*. St. Louis: Chalice, 1993.

Linthicum, Robert. *City of God, City of Satan: A Theology of the Urban Church*. Grand Rapids, MI: Zondervan, 1991.

Park, Andrew Sung. *Racial Conflict and Healing: An Asian-American Theological Perspective*. Mary Knoll, NY: Orbis Books, 1996.

Perkins, John. *Let Justice Roll Down*. Ventura, CA: Regal Books, 1976.

Rieger, Joerg. *Theology from the Belly of the Whale: A Fredrick Herzog Reader*. Harrisburg, PA: Trinity, 1999.

Saunders, Stanley P., and Charles L. Campbell. *The Word on the Street: Performing the Scriptures in the Urban Context*. Grand Rapids, MI: Eerdmans, 2000.

Schorr, Lisbeth, and Daniel. *Within Our Reach: Breaking the Cycle of Disadvantage*. New York: Anchor Books, 1988.

Short, John Rennie. *The Urban Order: An Introduction to Cities, Culture, and Power*. Oxford, United Kingdom: Blackwell Publishers, 1996.

Spina, Frank Anthony. *The Faith of the Outside: Exclusion and Inclusion in the Biblical Story.* Grand Rapids, MI: Eerdmans, 2005.

Takaki, Ronald. *A Different Mirror: A History of Multicultural America.* New York: Back Bay, 1993.

Tutu, Desmond. *No Future Without Forgiveness.* New York: Double Day, 2000.

Villafane, Eldin. *Seek the Peace of the City: Reflections on Urban Ministry.* Grand Rapids, MI: Eerdmans Press, 1995.

Volf, Miroslav. *Exclusion and Embrace: A Theological Explo-ration of Identity, Otherness, and Reconciliation.* Nashville: Abingdon, 1996.

Wallace Jim. *Faith Works: Lessons from the Life of an Activist Preacher.* New York: Random House, 2000.

Washington, James M., ed. *A Testament of Hope; The Essential Writings and Speeches of Martin Luther King Jr.* New York: Harper Collins, 1986.

West, Cornel. *Keeping Faith: Philosophy and Race in America.* New York: Routledge Classics, 1993.

_____. *Race Matters.* Boston: Beacon Press, 2001.

Yoder, John, Howard. *The Politics of Jesus.* Grand Rapids, MI: Eerdmans, 1972.

Web Sites

Bakke Graduate University
www.bgu.edu

Caffe Lusso Coffee Roasters
www.caffelusso.com

Center for Transforming Mission
www.CTMnet.org

New Horizons Ministries
www.nhmin.org

Soul Formation
www.SoulFormation.org

Street Bean Espresso
Streetbeanespresso.org

Accurate 2010

New Hope® Publishers is a division of WMU®, an
international organization that challenges Christian
believers to understand and be radically involved in God's
mission. For more information about WMU, go to www.
wmu.com. More information about New Hope books may
be found at www.newhopepublishers.com. New Hope
books may be purchased at your local bookstore.

If you've been blessed by this book, we would like to hear your story.
The publisher and author welcome your comments and
suggestions at: newhopereader@wmu.org.

Other ministry resources from
New Hope Publishers

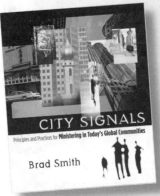

City Signals
Principles and Practices for Ministering in Today's Global Communities
Brad Smith
ISBN-10: 1-59669-045-3
ISBN-13: 978-1-59669-045-5

Faces in the Crowd
Reaching Your International Neighbor for Christ
Donna S. Thomas
ISBN-10: 1-59669-205-7
ISBN-13: 978-1-59669-205-3

Trolls & Truth
14 Realities About Today's Church That We Don't Want to See
Jimmy Dorrell
ISBN-10: 1-59669-010-0
ISBN-13: 978-1-59669-010-3

Available in bookstores everywhere

NEW HOPE
P U B L I S H E R S

For information about these books or any New Hope product, visit www.newhopepublishers.com.